Tales & Lies My Baba Told Me

A Memoir

by

Jennie TS Choban

Also by Jennie TS Choban:

NON-FICTION:

Kapusta or Cabbage (1995)

More Kapusta or Cabbage (2013)

PLAY:

So Write Already, Who's Stopping You?

Tales &Lies^ My Baba Told Me

A *her*storical memoir
part real, part fiction
the reader can choose what to believe

by

Jennie T S Choban
aka
Ewheniya Tschoban

Published by: JTS Press
Gibsons, BC
Contact: jennietsc@gmail.com

Library and Archives Canada Cataloguing in Publication
Choban, Jennie Ts, 1939-, author
Tales & Lies My Baba Told Me / Jennie Ts Choban

ISBN 978-0-9699556-2-7

I. Title.
TX723.5.U5C47 1995   641.5947 ' 71   C95-900387-8

First edition (Second Printing) published: August 2020, by JTS Press
Front cover illustration: Lauren E.R. Davidson

Dedicated to my grandson Sasha,
granddaughters Lauren and Athena.

Thank you, dear children,
for accepting this old lady into your lives.

TABLE OF CONTENTS

Introduction ix
Enter My Sister 1
Baba as a Nanny? No Way! 7
Enter Baba. 10
Blackberry Pies 18
Baba's Tale: Papa Had No Love For Stalin 23
Wash Your Hands. 27
Obey or Dis-obey 29
Bedtime Stories 33
The Number Games. 35
Diaper Service. 38
Quesadillas Coming Up. 40
Let it Snow. 44
Howl at the Moon 49
Baba's Tale: My Family. 53
Eat Cabbage & Poop All Day. 60
Awards. 64
Clouds 69
Baba and Wine 71
Daniel O'Donnell 74
Bobby Darin. 79
Ma! Did You Read the Instructions? 81
Coupons 83
Knit, Knit, Knit 85

Okay, Okay, You Don't Need to Ask Twice 90

Remembrance Day is Every Day 92

Baba's Tale: Nicholas and Taras 99

Mom! Help Me! 104

A Matching Pair 107

How do You Spell Dictionary? 110

Baba's Tale: My Chores 117

Be Careful What You Wish For 122

Thou Shalt Not Take God's Name in Vain 127

Baba's Tale: Religious Beliefs 133

Lobster 137

You Are One Mixed Up Kid 139

Baba's Tale: Prelude to War 143

Hair Cuts 153

Debates 155

High School 157

Baba's Tale: The Carpathian Mountains 165

INTRODUCTION

What's in a Memoir? When I wanted to write about the silly things I did three days a week for six years as a nanny to my grandchildren, it was very awkward to criticize myself - the way a grandkid would - without sounding obnoxious.

These are my tales, and some lies – sort of - of my life; but narrated by 17-year-old Alexandre Sasha, my grandson.

I was born in Ukraine and while World War II raged on, my family of eight fled our home and sought freedom – whatever that freedom might have been in the midst of war – in Germany.

We spoke no English when we immigrated to Canada in 1949. My parents, four older sisters and a brother all struggled at menial jobs. But the one thing that kept my family going was – freedom! Freedom to worship our Ukrainian Orthodox religion. Freedom to live a life without the fear of bombs and possible repatriation to Communist-occupied Ukraine.

Over the years, they all learned to speak some form of broken English - but they mostly valued the freedom of speaking our Ukrainian language at home and with friends.

As the youngest, I fought hard to *Kanadianize* myself, as my family embraced their old-world cultures.

After seven decades of living in Canada, I wanted my Canadian-born children and grandchildren to understand where I came from. But, how do I weave bits of my life when I was their age in Ukraine - fighting to stay alive while humanity fought tyranny –

with theirs?

Although I thank God that they hopefully will never experience what I did, perhaps they at least should know how fortunate they are living in Canada.

Tales & Lies includes my life as a child in flashbacks throughout the book. It's not a life I would wish on my grandkids – but I felt they would learn from my stories.

Never check an interesting fact...

– Howard Hughes

Never check facts in herstory...

– Jennie Choban

ENTER MY SISTER

When my parents announced they would need to hire a nanny to look after my six-month-old kid sister, the last person I expected to appear on our doorstep was – no, not Mary Poppins – but Baba! My mother's mother. My Ukrainian-born grandmother, Baba, who invaded our lives and proceeded to brainwash us with such far-fetched tales of her life in the old country, I often accused her of lying to us.

Had it been up to me, Mom would have stayed home with us until I was all grown up. But it wasn't up to me and no one even thought of asking my opinion.

This whole mess started when I was two years old and it seemed I wasn't enough for my parents to love so they decided to bring another kid into our family. Someone, they said, to keep me company so I wouldn't be lonely or worse, be raised as a spoiled brat.

I didn't know where this new brother – or no way, a *sister* – would come from, but the weirdest thing happened.

Mommy started getting fat.

"Sit gently on my stomach, Alex," Mom warned me whenever I wanted to cuddle in her lap. "We don't want to squish the baby."

Squish the baby? What baby? Other than me, there was no other baby in our home.

Over the next few months, Mom's stomach kept expanding bigger and bigger just like a balloon being inflated with air. Then it grew so big she could have lain face down on the floor and rolled around on it like she often did with her huge rubber exercise ball. Except now, she had her own built-in ball.

"Look, look, she's kicking!" Mom's eyes lit up as an arm or a leg tried to punch its way out of her stomach.

Actually, this whole thing of something or someone inside Mom's stomach freaked... me... out!

Was there an alien growing in her body? Yikes! Weird!

I really tried not to think about that part and as time went on I just had to sit next to Mom and watch as she lovingly patted her tummy.

Finally, when Mom's stomach grew to the size of a *giant* exercise ball Daddy drove her to St. Mary's Hospital.

She returned two days later – her tummy a lot flatter and a bundle in her arms. That bundle turned out to be my baby sister who invaded and disrupted my idyllic life as she made her presence in our home. What used to be just *my* home. Now also hers.

And sadly, I soon found out that I was no longer the most important person in my parents' lives.

Actually, I kind of looked forward to having a sibling. But the fact that I got a sister instead of a brother was not my choice. But I told myself maybe it's good that I have a kid sister to beat up on. And snitch on. And possibly blame her for all my wrongdoings. After all, not everything bad that happened around the house should be blamed on me. Right?

They named my kid sister Athena – after some beautiful Greek goddess in Ancient Mythology. Like I cared.

But my parents did and everyone who looked at my sister thought she was just the greatest thing ever. Sometimes they even paid more attention to that baby than they did to Tiger Lily, our tabby cat. So the cat and I became best friends. Not by choice – but by necessity.

I thought The Kid – what I sometimes called my sister instead of by her proper name – looked like a big blob of flesh. She had deep brown eyes with pitch black hair flying every which way. She often made weird faces. And the first time Mom said, "Look, look, our baby is smiling," Dad frowned as he sniffed the air and announced that it was probably just gas.

Taking care of a new baby took up most of Mom's time, so quite often I was left to find my own ways of entertaining myself. I loved building various objects with my abundant supply of Lego blocks and spent a lot of time practising printing letters and numbers with crayons and colourful pencils on sheets of paper.

Several times a day, my sister gravitated towards Mommy's chest and lay there for a long time, sometimes making funny slurping noises. And when Mom placed her face down over her shoulder, Mom would gently pat the back until she'd burp once... and again. *Good girl*, Mom always said and when she was satisfied that no gas remained in her baby, she laid her in the crib. As if needing a replacement for Mom's breast to pacify her, Athena shoved the thumb of her right hand into her mouth, closed her eyes and promptly fell into a deep satisfying sleep. And there she stayed in La La Land for hours.

Mom said that if our baby sleeps for at least two hours after feeding, it's a good sign that her milk is rich and the baby is pretty healthy and happy. And she, the mother, can get a couple of hours of rest. Unless her older brother – meaning me – becomes too demanding for attention. Which I must admit happened almost always.

When I asked how can Mom feed my sister without a bottle or

cup to hold the milk, she tried to explain what breastfeeding was all about – but at first it went way over my head. But when she said that I was also fed this way until I was more than a year old and was weaned onto a bottle of store-bought formula to replace a mother's natural milk, it was another freak-out moment for me. To think I could be fed this way was a little disturbing until I was much older and read books where baby animals feeding off their mothers was the only way to give them proper nourishment. A natural way of sustaining life.

The first time I watched Mom change diapers, I gagged. When Mom reminded me that I also was once a baby, I yelled back, "Don't tell me! I don't want to know!"

I was fully trained before three. So if I ever did go through the diaper stage, as gross as it was, I managed to put it out of my mind – for…ever.

Before long, my sister grew on me. When she wasn't sleeping in her crib, she'd lay around on the living room floor, padded with a thick soft blanket with colourful patterns of *Winnie the Pooh* – and *Tigger* too – that Mom saved after I grew out of it.

At times, I actually enjoyed playing with Athena. She always had this happy laugh when I twirled her around on a blanket on the floor – like a spinning top.

Months passed and when she started to crawl, there was no stopping her. She was a wild baby, getting into everything.

Once she tried to stick her head through the gate at the top of the stairs in the kitchen. Lucky for her, her head was too big to fit between the slats. So instead, she turned over, slid backwards on her stomach and stuck her two legs through the slats. Then she screamed and screamed until Mom pulled her out.

Athena was forever being lifted from one possible hazardous place and put into an area of safety. Apparently, my parents experienced that with me too and often Mom would say, "Alex, remember when you were her age and you did..." As much as I wanted to, I could not remember any of those events when I was her age.

My parents did not believe in playpens. Too confining. Let the baby roam around without feeling enclosed like in a prison.

* * * * *

I also did not have a playpen when I was growing up, but there are several photographs of me standing and sitting and playing with toys – in a cardboard box. Big enough for me to lie down on the bottom. I was not quite one when Baba visited us for a few weeks and when I started walking, she said she got tired of chasing me around the house. So she made me a playpen out of a huge paper towel carton she got from the grocery store. Actually, I was much safer and enjoyed playing with toys inside that box. However, as soon as my parents came home, the box went onto the balcony and again I was free to roam around.

* * * * *

So, my sister was free to crawl anywhere she wanted and many times she'd make her way over to me – maybe looking for a playmate?

My silly methods of teasing my baby sister often annoyed my parents with orders to *stop hurting your sister... she's not a toy!* The first time she managed to stand up, she held onto the couch and when she was about to take a step, I stuck my foot out and tripped her. Her fat body plunked onto the hardwood floor, face down, and out came a shrieking wail.

"You could have broken her nose!" Mom yelled at me.

Maybe not. Maybe I lucked in because Mom once read to me from Dr. Spock's *Baby Book* that at that point in a baby's bodily development the nose was not quite bone, just some cartilage.

"If you ever trip your sister on her face again, I just might do the same to you," she warned me. "See if you like having your face hit the floor."

I never wanted to find out if I liked having my face squashed on the hardwood floor, possibly breaking my fully-developed nose, so I devised other ways to bug The Kid.

My parents were happy. Our new baby was happy. And I was satisfied that maybe a sister was better than no brother. We were one middle-sized happy family of government-approved quota. Two parents, two children – male and female – an ideal millionaire's family. And one cat – fixed.

Everything was fine until Mom, an award-winning pastry chef, announced she wanted to open her own pastry shop in a store-front, a five-minute walk down the street from where we lived.

BABA AS A NANNY? NO WAY!

While living in Vancouver, British Columbia, Mom became a professional pastry chef. She had won awards for her pastry creations and worked at high-end caterers whose clientele appreciated the work effort and the many organic ingredients that went into creating a variety of baked goods. After working for two years as Head Pastry Chef at an elegant Italian restaurant, Mom decided to take a chance on running her own shop.

Shortly after, we moved to Gibsons – what Baba described as a rinky-dink town – on the Sunshine Coast. Mom searched out a spot overlooking the Marina and rented an out-of-business shop complete with baking ovens. When Dad agreed to support Mom in her new business, a lease was signed and *The Sweet Chef* was born.

* * * * *

Five years later, Mom was approached by a developer to expand into a chain of shops but decided she wanted a life of regular hours and to devote more time to her children, play soccer and help run Dad's Aikido Do Jo, so she closed the shop. Then she wrote the exam for a Real Estate Agent License and joined Dad in his business.

* * * * *

With Mom working five days a week at her bakery, my sister and I would go to daycare for two days and Mom would stay home and look after us for two days. That left three more days of each week of every month for the next six years – until Athena and I would attend school full-time – to have someone look after us. Three days a week, from morning 'til night, a stranger would come into our home and become our nanny.

"What if?" Mom discussed with Dad, "my Mom moved out here from Ontario?"

"Your mother?" Dad questioned her. "You want your mother to give up her single life and move out here to look after our kids?"

"Why not?" Mom said. "She's always wanted to live in the west. And anyway, she really doesn't have much of an exciting life now that her four-year relationship with what's-his-name came to an abrupt end. Her stuff has been in storage for the past year that she's been living with my brother. Just call the movers and she's here in no time."

"Maybe we should ask your brother what kind of nanny your mother was for their baby before we decide," Dad said with a smirk.

* * * * *

To be fair, Baba had planned to retire here, in British Columbia, permanently. When I was two-and-a-half years old she drove out here to test out the area and for six months she lived in a secluded B&B in a forest where deer roamed freely. Once, we even stood right next to a baby deer as it nibbled on the vegetation in a garden. Twice a week Baba would come by and take me to a playground, the park, long nature walks and drop-ins at Strong

Start at the elementary school.

Most of the time we got along, until she ordered me to do this and don't do that and I'd start crying and threaten to tell Mom and Dad that Baba was mean to me, then she'd bribe me with a treat and everything was well again. At the end of each day, I was back with Mom and Dad. So most of my memories were mainly of having fun with Baba. However, when I was a year older, I did not want my old Grandma – a Ukrainian Baba – for a nanny.

* * * * *

Baba must have gotten a half-decent reference from Uncle Dee and Aunt Kin where she lived for one year as nanny for my six-month-old cousin Lauren. Or maybe they wanted to rid her from Ontario and Vancouver was the farthest, without leaving Canada.

I just wished I were old enough for Kindergarten so I could be with other kids and out of the house during the day – away from Baba.

But a three-year-old kid had no say in adult decisions. And so, without even asking for my approval, for the next several years Baba ruled our lives as my sister's Nanny – and mine by default. Yikes!

ENTER BABA

So, Baba left her boring – her words, not mine – life in Ontario, and moved into a one-bedroom condo. Just ten minutes walking distance from our home – or eight, if she jogged part way. But if she ran out of breath and had to stop for a rest on the curb, then her time would be doubled.

And, when Mom really needed her at the last minute, Baba would say, "I could drive over there in three minutes, tops."

"Hello," she'd announce, unlocking our front door. "It's me."

As if we didn't know.

"I'm here."

Now go away, I often wanted to say.

"Good morning, kiddies," she addressed us.

Once she showed up in her pyjamas. "I overslept... just a little bit. But don't worry, I can always go home later to shower and change into decent clothes. I'm in and out of the car. Who's looking at the way I dress? No one here I know."

Lucky for Baba by the time she came over Mom was already at work and Dad was on his way out and paid no attention to what Baba wore. Later, she drove to her place for a shower and change of clothes.

"We wouldn't want your parents' friends to see me walking around the mall in my bedclothes," she told us, as if we cared how she dressed.

Baba looked like what a grandmother should look like. Round

10

face with hardly any wrinkles except when she grinned. She had short hair with streaked highlights. Because, she said, her mousy brown hair that was not yet grey to give it some body, made her look unattractive.

She stood five feet two inches and was kind of overweight – chunky, her preferred term. Shortly after she moved here, she joined an exercise class with Mom. In a year or so, she lost about 20 pounds and then stopped going. Said she had enough of those skinny girls puffing and huffing in their tight bodysuits.

Then Baba told us about when Mom was just a baby and Baba joined a Fitness Club. And once a week Baba went off to enjoy a few hours away from family chores.

"Back then," Baba said, "I weighed one hundred and ten pounds and wore size six clothes. And running around after your brother and you all day long gave me enough exercise that I didn't need to go to the fitness spa."

"So, why did you waste your money and time to go?" Mom asked.

"To get out of the house!" Baba said. "After the class, a few of the girls would go out for coffee or soda. No husbands and no kids. Back then, wives did not have the freedom that you enjoy now. But an exercise class was great for us girls who needed to get away from it all. Once a week. Something to look forward to. It was great to gab and complain about our lives without getting in trouble with the husbands.

"Anyway, one evening after the exercise class, one woman – very over-weight and definitely needed the workout – eyed me and up down and said, 'Why are you here?' And without even thinking I blurted out, 'I'm what you're supposed to look like.'"

"Did she belt you one?" Mom laughed. "I would have."

"Nah. But she always looked at me kinda funny after that and stayed as far away from me as possible," Baba said. Then she looked down onto her protruding belly and realizing that she was now what that over-weight woman was then, she shrugged her shoulders, "Oh well, can't change the past and maybe I'm being punished for that remark."

Baba's real reason for quitting was that she hated organized exercise classes. "I really hate being told how to bend down... four more... three more... two more... and relax... and breathe out."

She said that running around after us was enough daily exercise. "Especially with all the walking and lifting and schlepping your sister like a sack of potatoes – first the weight of ten pounds, then twenty, then even more."

So, after a daily workout with us kids, all she needed was her couch at home and a glass of wine.

Baba had piercing blue eyes. And at times when she admonished us they were so bulging and threatening that if we didn't obey I'm sure she could have zapped us into another dimension.

Other than that, she was normal except at times her face took on a look of still suffering. I had no idea what that meant, but years later when she delved into her past and regaled us with stories of her childhood in Germany during and after World War II, the meaning of the term 'still suffering' became somewhat clearer.

So, three days a week Baba was at our house, looking after my dumb baby sister. I was also there, but had no say in the matter. Not a word of objection was allowed.

If that wasn't enough of our Baba hanging around, she also looked after us three evenings a week, while my parents taught Aikido at their Martial Arts Dojo.

Over the next several years, we had our fill of Baba. And to be fair, I'm sure she had enough of us. After all, she was in her late sixties. And, maybe a little too old to be running after us kids.

One time I heard a friend of Mom's say to her, "You're so lucky to have your mother close by. Mine would never look after my kids. Not even for a week-end."

"Yeah, right," Mom replied, rolling her eyes. There were times when Mom and Baba did not agree on how to raise us kids, and some harsh words were exchanged. Then they made up and everything was back to normal. Until the next time they found something else to quarrel over.

I suppose we could have been worse off. A lazy nanny, who'd neglect us. Maybe raiding our fridge and gorging herself, ignoring us so we got into whatever kind of mischief we chose. I guess that could have been fun, but after a while even we needed some sort of order and stability. Not that Baba was *that* stable, I thought.

Yet, Baba was no Mary Poppins who was young and flew through the air with an umbrella as a parachute. Baba was our grandmother – like it or lump it! Definitely not a choice I would have made for a nanny, but for a grandmother I gave her a passing grade.

"When you're old enough to look after your sister," she said reminding me that her nanny job was temporary, "I'm going North... to Alaska." And then she sang a few bars of the song Johnny Horton made famous way back in her younger days.

"What are you going to do there?" I asked. "Live in an igloo?"

"Adventure, my boy!" she replied. "I'll know what's there, when I get there."

From the start, I begged Mom not to leave us with Baba.

"I don't want Baba here all the time," I cried when Mom came home from work. "I want you to stay home with me. Anyway, who's going to feed my baby sister?"

"Baba, of course," Mom said.

I'm freaking out! I didn't want to see my baby sister leaning against Baba's chest to be fed like she did with Mommy. Gross!

When Baba went to feed Athena I turned away – I did not want to see this, but when she held a small bottle with a nipple, it was full of milk. When I asked her why she doesn't feed the baby like Mom did, she laughed and kept on laughing and when she finally stopped laughing and while wiping her eyes she tried to explain that no one except mothers feed their kids that way. Phew! At least I would never be subjected to that disgusting scene I had pictured.

As the days and then weeks went on I was not happy to have Baba with us all that time. Each time she appeared she took over my life and I knew for sure if she did not leave, permanently, I would be driven to insanity. Like, real insanity. Not just the imaginary type. Like when I threw a temper tantrum and Mom told me to stop acting up.

What if I become so distraught over Baba's interference in my life, they may have to put me in an Insane Asylum? To be cloistered with all those other crazies, who really are mentally unbalanced, if through no fault of their own. They're the ones doctors should focus on. Not me. The possibility of my confinement at the Funny Farm would not even be an issue and completely avoidable – if Baba would not play nanny to my baby sister.

"You have no choice, dear," Mom said every time I complained. Then she'd shrug her shoulders and hug me tight. "Come on kiddo, Baba's not *that* bad. Anyway, before you know it, you'll soon be in school and then all grown up and you won't need anyone to look after you."

Really? Before I know it? What was Mom's definition of 'before you know it'? One year? Two years? I was three at the time. Before I know would not be for another decade! Yikes!

"I'll run away from home," I threatened.

Of course running away was not an option. Where would a three-year-old run? In the backyard? Next door to a neighbour? Only to be dragged back and be chastised by you-know-who.

Since leaving home was not a solution to my dilemma of ridding myself of Baba, I made life as miserable for her as I possibly could. I did everything to annoy her. Throwing tantrums were mostly ignored.

"When your brother gets over his fit, we'll go out," she'd announce to my sister as if a six-month-old blob of a baby knew what this was all about. It's like having a conversation with a doll. "Then maybe he can work off his frustrations in the park."

When she told me I had to eat my celery sticks first before I could have the two cookies she placed on a plate, I accidentally on purpose threw a glass of milk onto the floor.

"You're lucky it's plastic, young man," Baba said, removing a mop out of the closet and proceeding to clean the floor.

"And don't *never ever waste* food again," she raised her voice, peering at me with her piercing blue eyes.

It turned out that Baba dug her own grave, as grownups say when one offers something possibly in the form of a gift, not knowing that the recipient would use it against them.

From the time I was able to hold a crayon in my hand, I scribbled on any piece of paper in the house.

When Baba saw my artwork on the hall wall, she went to the Dollar Store and bought me a special scribbler. On the inside of the cover all the letters of the alphabet were listed – capital and lower case. In print form and in cursive.

Daily, I'd sit at the dining table, block out Baba's voice as much as possible, practise printing and immerse myself into a world of the written word.

"How do you spell 'Baba'?" I asked, after I learned how to print most of the letters.

She'd reply, enunciating each letter, pausing a second after each one, so I'd have enough time to print it.

"And how do you spell 'yell'?"

Again, she'd comply. With the same patience – "y... e... l... l..."

"What about 'mean'?" I continued.

"....what about 'nice'?"

".... and 'not'?"

"I would suggest you use the dictionary, but first you need to know how to spell the word before you can look it up. English language just boggles the mind," Baba said after I kept pestering her to spell out words. "When you get older, I'll let you use SpellCheck on my laptop and not bother me with all your silly questions."

I don't think she ever clued in and with pure innocence helped me correctly spell her possible demise. After I perfected all the letters, maybe I could write a tell-all of Baba's so-called kid-sitting. What would Mom say then, eh? Mom will take my side and never stick up for her mother again.

"You should see how well your son is printing," Baba reported each evening, as soon as either one of my parents appeared at the front door.

"Although some of the words he's writing are not to my liking, but what do I know?" Baba snitched on me, as she walked out the door murmuring, "Kids nowadays – who knows, eh?"

Little did she know that one day I might use those words against her. And little did I know that she would get me back. And good.

But for the next couple of years, we both played the game of gotcha.

She got to rule over me. And I got to tattle on her as soon as she disappeared out the front door.

BLACKBERRY PIES

Baba's discovery of wild blackberry bushes that grew everywhere drove her into a gathering frenzy. And best, it wouldn't cost her anything. Not a single penny. Well, actually, she never counted the gas she spent driving around the coast looking for bushes with ripe berries. Especially those that were not part of someone's private property.

Her first year on the coast, Baba filled our freezer with blackberries.

Every few days – when she was not looking after us – she'd come by with an *It's just me...* as she entered the front door and went down into the lower level of the house to a freezer in the storage room. And deposited another batch of plastic containers of blackberries.

"We need room for tomatoes in our freezer," Mom reminded Baba that we couldn't live on blackberries alone.

"Fine," Baba said, sounding sort of rejected. "Anyway, the season is over."

"Good," Mom said.

"Until next year," Baba grinned and then mumbled, "If I'm still around."

Mom and Baba made their own favourite concoction of pure alcohol and berries in large wine bottles.

"In six months," Baba said, "we'll have our own sweet liqueur. The best you ever tasted."

I never did get to drink any, on account of I was nowhere near legal drinking age. But I did sample a few drops of what tasted like a very sweet cough syrup.

Over the winter and spring, every two or three weeks, Baba would bring a huge baking dish filled with berries and a streusel crumble.

When Mom asked why she didn't make pies for a change, Baba's reply of, "I'm not a pastry chef, like you. My attempt at pastry making always turns too crumbly, so why bother with freezing the dough and then rolling it with hopes it doesn't turn into crumble – which it does almost always."

"Blackberries are ripe," Baba announced in mid-August.

"Great," Mom said. "I need enough for about two dozen pies."

Mom baked a lot of special event cakes. Weddings, birthdays, whatever a client would order.

"You need enough for how many?" Baba frowned and shook her head. "Do you have any idea how long it will take me to gather enough blackberries so you can make two dozen pies? Not to mention the gas I will use driving around the Coast looking for bushes with ripe berries?"

"Do the best you can, Mother. But I need them within the next few days. If you can't, I'll have to order from the supplier."

"Well, I could use two dollars a pie," Baba said. "I'm sure you have to pay at least double that from the supplier."

At this point Mom did her usual shaking her head and eyes up at the ceiling thing she often did when her Mother ranted on about whatever the topic of discussion was at the time.

"Hope it doesn't rain tomorrow," Baba said. "And if it's too sunny, it's blinding."

"Ma, just wear your sunglasses."

"If I wear my sunglasses it's too dark and I can't tell whether the berries are ripe or not. Your bride may end up with green blackberry pies," Baba said.

Next day, blanket on grass, Athena played with toys and every once in a while you heard "ouch, ouch," as Baba gathered ripe blackberries from prickly bushes that grew wildly along the side of a park next to our school.

I was kicking a soccer ball around the field and when I tried to play catch with my sister, she missed every time I sent the ball her way. But when I bonked her on the head, she screamed as if I really hurt her and Baba screamed at me, "What's wrong with you, kid? Stop hurting your sister!"

"Not my fault she's not catching it."

"She just learned how to walk," Baba said. "How can you expect her to play catch with a ball?"

Finally, when two large stainless steel bowls are filled with berries and securely tucked into plastic bags, Baba hoisted Athena under one arm and I carried the blanket and a tote of toys to the car.

The next day, Mom is off work and while we're having dinner, the front door opens. "It's just me," Baba said.

She climbed up the stairs into the kitchen and deposited another huge batch of berries that she had spent all day gathering from bushes in the neighbourhood that she previously had not pilfered. More than enough so Mom could complete the order for the wedding dessert table.

"Stay for dinner," Mom said. "We're having that mac and cheese you made for us yesterday."

"No thanks," Baba said. "Already ate. On my way now to the library for my book club meeting with the old farts that have nothing better to do than analyze what they remember reading about – whatever – the previous month."

"What are you reading, Baba?" I ask. She often said that she wished she had more time to read instead of looking after us brats, but if she goes to a regular book club she probably gets her fill of literature and just likes to complain about things that really don't affect her that much.

"A novel about some events during the war – the WWII. Except it's written by a woman who knows how to do research and interview her Grandparents, but has never experienced what war is all about," Baba said.

"What's a WWII?" I asked.

"You want to know about WWII, kid?" she said, shaking her head. "You don't want to know about The Big War. When you get older, maybe I'll tell you all about it."

"Love you," Mom said and hugged Baba before she left the kitchen.

"Love you too," Baba said, and then before she closed the front door on her way out, she yelled, "And don't forget, you owe me for the pies – two dollars apiece."

* * * * *

Over the years, I questioned Baba about her family – my great grandparents and great aunts and uncle. Stuff about their lives before she immigrated to Canada. And each time she dismissed it. Then one day, as she was going home she handed me a manuscript. A stack of typed pages of what turned out to be, as she often said she would write, her memoir. Life before she came to Canada. She was nine at the time, so I guess she felt I was old enough – at ten – to understand some grown-up stuff.

Every so often I pulled the three-ring loose leaf binder that sat on the bottom shelf of a bookcase in our family room and flipped through the pages. Didn't quite understand what it all meant but by the time I got halfway through high school, I finally finished reading it. Of course, most of it, I didn't believe. It was somewhat like the stuff we saw on the news of war and refugees. And death.

BABA'S TALE
– UKRAINE –
1944

PAPA HAD NO LOVE FOR STALIN

My Papa hated Stalin. And even though the two men never met, Papa had good reason to despise the Soviet dictator. Especially after that morning when Stalin's soldiers shot Mr. Petrenko.

And while Papa stood by helpless, he wept as Mr. Petrenko lay dead on the ground.

Papa was a religious man, who loved life and his family. The thought of harming a human made him sick to his stomach. But after watching his neighbour and best friend murdered right there in front of his eyes, Papa realized that only Stalin's death would stop him from killing another human being.

Papa chastised God for allowing such a monster to live and he begged God to remove the communist leader off the face of the earth.

But then, there wasn't one Christian in all of Ukraine who didn't pray that death would come to Joseph Stalin. And the sooner, the better.

Who was this man, that Papa hated so? How can one man be so powerful that on his command millions ceased to exist?

STALIN

Joseph Vissarionovich Dzhugashvili (1879-1953) was better known to the world as Joseph Stalin. An evil Russian dictator of the Soviet Union, he had a deep hatred for the Ukrainian people.

During the early 1930s, Ukraine lost its struggle for independence under Stalin's rule and became part of the Soviet Union. Stalin was threatened by their religious and cultural beliefs and proceeded to destroy as many Ukrainians as he could. He confiscated the rich soil from the prosperous peasants and orchestrated a famine to purge Ukraine of what he considered undesirables.

Minstrels, more commonly known as Kobzars, were mostly blind musicians who played stringed instruments known as Kobza and Bandura, and sang of a free Ukraine. Hundreds of them were executed in an effort to destroy the Ukrainian culture.

During the famine between 1932-1934, some nine million Ukrainians either starved to death, were executed, or sent to Siberia and labour camps as slaves.

The surviving Ukrainians lived under the Communist rule, on whatever Stalin's government deemed necessary to survive. Stalin controlled the rich wheat fields that once belonged to the farmers. The dream of working towards a better life was no longer an option to the Ukrainian people.

By the summer of 1939, Adolf Hitler – dictator of Nazi Germany – was on a quest to rule all of Europe and started by occupying Poland.

Stalin was not giving up his control and retaliated, resulting in the breakout of World War II.

As the war escalated, thousands of Ukrainians fled their homeland seeking a better life in Western Europe. But freedom eluded many of them as Soviets captured and returned the runaways back to Ukraine. Young men were forced into the Soviet Army to fight Hitler as Stalin battled for control of Europe.

Stalin ordered his armies to impound farms and homes, deeming them as collective farms. All able-bodied men and women were banished to collective farms and work camps. Men and women were forced to cultivate the farms that once were their homes. Cattle and farm animals no longer belonged to the farmer. Vegetables, fruit, corn and wheat were sold and the money turned over to Stalin's communist government.

Peasants were sent to work in factories, building ammunition for Stalin to use on their own people.

Ukrainians would live the rest of their lives as slaves in their own homes.

Any Ukrainian who refused to abide by Stalin's orders was shot to death.

Just like Mr. Petrenko was on that morning of July 1944.

How can one man have the power to destroy so many good people?

Stalin was an evil man who set out to conquer all of Europe and then rule all the countries collectively as one communist nation. Which meant no man, woman or child would have any freedom to live a life of their choosing. And for the rest of their days, they would be slaves to Stalin's regime.

While the war between Hitler and Stalin raged on, the Soviet Army continued to destroy Ukraine.

To accomplish total occupation of Europe, Stalin sought to control all forms of culture. Poets and writers who praised their freedom fighters and wrote that one day Ukraine would be free of communist rule, were exiled to prisons.

It was no wonder Papa hated Stalin. For Stalin loved power and people were dispensable. Especially Christian Ukrainians who believed in God and refused to acknowledge Stalin as the almighty ruler.

Christians were forbidden to worship God. Religious icons confiscated and churches destroyed.

Stalin ordered books be burned, thereby wiping out any historical reference of Ukraine and its people.

We lived in Storozinetz, a small city in the Province of Chernovtzi, east of Romania and the Carpathian Mountains.

I first heard that evil man's name shortly after my fifth birthday in the summer of 1944.

When Papa learned that Stalin's Soviet soldiers raided another farm and burned homes in a nearby village, his eyes bugged out, his teeth clenched tight, as he slammed a fist into the wall.

Which made Mama shake her head, "Save your strength, Dyonisis. You won't rid of him by wrecking the house."

The whole town was in a frenzy. For days, the messages were passed on from farm to farm. The Russians are coming... The Russians are coming...

There was no telling when the Soviet army would descend upon us. And then what?

"Only God knows," Papa said. "But we must be ready. It's Stalin at his worst and if we don't get ready now, we might never get another chance."

And so, our family prepared to evacuate our home.

For days, we separated our belongings into "we take" and "we leave" piles. All the while sniffing away tears. There sure were many tears shed in the days that followed. The grownups must have known something I didn't. For once we left, they saw the possibility of total abandonment of our home, our town. Even our country.

WASH YOUR HANDS

"Hey, which one of you two didn't flush the toilet?" Baba asked.

When she didn't get the answer she expected she continued, "Are you both going to ignore me? One of you better go into that bathroom and flush that toilet!"

Okay, it definitely was not my two-year-old sister who was still in diapers and perhaps Baba didn't want to come right out and accuse me of not being mindful of her training so she called both of us out.

I should have done it in the first place, so reluctantly I stopped watching television and got up off the couch. Clunk, I pushed the handle, the yellow liquid disappeared into the sewers and I returned to the living room.

"Did you wash your hand?" Baba yelled from the kitchen.

Hand? Wash my hand? Only one hand, not both?

"I didn't go to the bathroom," I yelled back.

"But you touched the handle," she yelled again. "Always wash your hands before leaving the bathroom!"

And thus she proceeded to train us on how to wash our hands, after we used the toilet. Properly. According to Baba.

"Right hand wipes and left hand, the clean one, flushes," she rattled on her instructions. "That way, there are no germs passed on from one hand to another. Then, both hands get a vigorous washing with soap."

Always she stood over us as we soaped up our hands and squished the foam underneath our fingernails, digging out dirt and germs.

Once she told us of living on their farm in Ukraine, where water had to be drawn from a well into a bucket connected to a long rope and heated up in a cauldron on a ledge of a cement oven in their home.

Another time, we heard of her years in a Displaced Persons Camp during World War II, when there was hardly any clean water to drink, never mind bathe in. As a child, a weekly wash in a tub of murky water was a luxury. Even though all five sisters – Baba being the youngest – used the same wash water. The cleanest sister bathed first in the fresh water and the dirtiest one got in last. Each one taking her turn scrubbing away the weekly dirt and leaving it behind for the next bather.

When I got older and she saw me take a book into the bathroom, well, all hell broke loose.

"You'd better make sure you put that book on the floor before you wipe!" she said. "And wash your hands before you pick up that book off the floor."

Baba was a germ-a-phobic and spent a lot of time disinfecting and washing our books. Especially those we brought home from the Library. Every book, outside and inside covers, got wiped down with a facecloth soaked in anti-bacterial spray. She always ignored the note the library pasted onto the clear plastic cover that read: Do Not Wash Books.

OBEY OR DIS-OBEY

At least once a month after Baba had gone home I'd run crying to Mom that I no longer wanted to be abused by Baba and that she should be replaced by a *nice* nanny.

Then Mom would phone her mother for more discussions on how to sit my unruly sister and out-of-control me.

"But he's just a kid," Mom said into the phone. "Yeah, I know it's hard on you." She listened and listened to Baba's explanation of why I snitched on her.

"Well... he needs more time to react to your orders," Mom said. I had no idea what lies Baba was telling Mom, but I knew they were definitely lies.

"Well, okay, maybe you don't think they are orders, but he does. He's just a kid, Ma. Yeah, I know you know that, but still..."

Pause.

"Well, if that's what really happened," Mom said, "you don't need to apologize."

Pause.

"Well, okay, it's up to you... apologize," she said and handed me the phone.

I shook my head yelling, "No! No! No!"

"He won't talk to you, Mom," Mom said into the phone.

Pause.

"So," Mom said, "can you still sit tomorrow night so we can go out to dinner?"

To which I imagined Baba replied with her favourite and

often-used phrase – *of course, why wouldn't I sit my grandkids? They're my flesh and blood.*

Then Mom ended the conversation with her usual, "Okay, see you Mom... love you, too."

The next evening, Mom and Dad walked out the front door and Baba walked in.

"Hi kids, it's me, I'm here."

My kid sister yelled "Yeah!" and ran to Baba, wrapping herself around her legs in a big hug.

I remained at the kitchen table, copying lists of food items from a Greek take-out menu for a restaurant I might one day open.

"How are you doing, kid?" she said and placed a Reese's Cup beside my notebook.

"Okay," I said, as I pulled apart the wrapper and took a bite of the peanut butter chocolate.

"I'm sorry about all that yelling yesterday," she said behind me.

I didn't look at her. I'm not about to forgive her even though I know she's bribing me with a treat.

Okay, so maybe it was my fault and I didn't check for cars before stepping off the sidewalk like she always taught us. Look right – look left – cars – wait... no cars – cross – rapidly – no, no, don't run so you don't trip, fall down and get run over by a speeding car.

Maybe she did save my life, but she grabbed me so hard I thought she would rip my arm out of my shoulder. Then she yelled at me so loud she drove me to tears. She didn't have to send me to my room – I went willingly just to get away from her and wait until Mom or Dad came home. Then I would give them my side of the story.

"You almost broke my arm," I said, recalling how hard she grabbed my wrist and dragged me back onto the sidewalk.

"How many times did we go over the rules of safely crossing the street?" she said. "Anyway, better a possible broken arm than a dead you in a casket with everyone sobbing because you didn't look both ways before running into the traffic."

"Geez, Baba, you don't have to scare me like that."

"I guess I'm getting too old for this kid sitting," Baba defended herself. "Oh well, look at it this way... in another year you'll be in school fulltime. I won't be around, well, not that much anyway. Your sister will still need someone to look after her when your parents are working, but at least you won't."

Hooray, I wanted to cheer, but before I got a chance to utter the word, I felt her hands grab my head from behind and then she plunked a loud smack-a-roo on top of my head.

Then she sniffed my hair a couple times and said, "You could use a good shampoo, you know."

A couple days later on our way to the park for our outing, she told us of a kid who got off the school bus and darted across the street without checking both ways. And to validate the story, she drove us to that bus stop and as she slowed the car, she crossed herself and pointed to a bouquet of flowers on the grassy spot of that horrible accident.

"There are no second chances in car accidents, kid," Baba said, driving away. "It's either death or worse, spend the rest of your life in a wheelchair."

That did it for me. From then on, whenever I was about to cross the street, I felt her imaginary tug on my arm as I checked both ways.

And, for the next few weeks everything was fine between us. Until I got tired of being a good kid and drove Baba around the bend. Again.

BEDTIME STORIES

From the time Baba started looking after us, Mom often reminded her to read a story to Athena at bedtime.

"Why am I reading to a baby?" Baba said. "There's no way she understands why *Goldilocks* snuck into *The Three Bears'* house."

"My baby understands more than you think," Mom insisted. "Just do it, Mother. Please."

Three evenings a week, it was a bedtime ritual. Athena was in her crib all covered up, thumb in mouth, her tiny hand clutching her favourite stuffed puppy. I lay on my stomach on a huge pillow on the floor, while Baba sat in a rocking chair and read a book. When Athena got a regular bed, I'd get comfortable on top of the covers while Baba propped a pillow behind her against the headboard. Short picture books would be read to the end. The longer ones Baba would read halfway through or stopped when she got tired of reading.

We had our favourites that we read over and over again. Many picture books, *ABCs* by Dr. Seuss, and *Five Little Monkeys* we never tired of.

When Baba read Beatrice Potter's *Peter Rabbit* she always omitted a part she found horrible and could not understand why it was written into a children's book.

"You missed the part where the father rabbit got put into a pie." Athena removed her thumb out of her mouth to remind Baba.

Baba hated that part and always skipped it.

As I aged, my choice for books changed and I preferred to read to myself in my own bed with Tiger Lily comfortably sleeping on top of the covers.

One evening, I heard a lot of laughter from Athena's room.

"What's so funny?" I asked.

"Baba's reading about Mom's cat Daisy using Baba's unshaved legs as a scratch pole," Athena said laughing. So, I jumped onto the bed and listened as more silly stories were read from *Kapusta or Cabbage* – a cookbook Mom and Baba wrote together years ago, about the many battles between them as Mom was growing up.

"Am I in the book?" I said.

"Nope. You weren't even thought of back then."

"Maybe you should write one about me," I said, feeling sort of left out.

"Oh, Alex, you haven't lived long enough for a book," Baba said, dismissing my idea and then, as an afterthought, she said, "Maybe when you get older."

THE NUMBER GAMES

When I was one, Baba bought me a block of foamy numbers. Cut-outs made of thick foam with numbers from zero to nine, in various colours. Those foamy numbers went everywhere with me, even to bed. I held onto them as if they were a part of me. When they became cracked or broken from overuse, Baba would go to the Dollar Store and buy a replacement.

When I was two, the whole family went to Uncle Dee and Aunt Kin's wedding in the Dominican Republic.

I was going to be the ring bearer. Baba bought me a real kid's black tuxedo with white shirt, a bow tie, long pants and a pair of dark shorts, in case the weather got too hot. Which it did.

On top of my parents' dresser is a wedding album of photos Baba took of our trip.

There are pictures of me, dressed in the tuxedo, walking along the grassy aisle towards the altar where Uncle Dee waited for his bride-to-be. In my hands I held – not the pillow with the rings – but my foamy numbers. Another picture is of Mom holding me in her arms and carrying me further up the aisle. Behind her, was my granddad – carrying the pillow with the rings. I was not about to relinquish my foamy numbers for anyone's wedding day.

From the time I was two, whenever I went for walks along the street with Baba I always read off the numbers on the houses.

"Hey, Baba, there's no number 1063 or 1065," I said, after

reading the addresses of 1064 and 1066 of two houses next to each other.

"Look across the street," she said.

"Why are the odd ones on the other side?" I asked.

"I don't know who came up with that numbering system, but maybe when you get older and want to know more, you can do some research."

When I learned how to add and subtract numbers, I loved going to George Park – that's what I called it – the George Park. A small private grassy cemetery, surrounded by a tall steel fence and a brass statue of the founder of our town, George Gibson. Only he and a few relatives were buried there.

I wasn't interested in the cemetery part, especially after Baba freaked me out by reminding me not to walk over the graves where the dead bodies were buried. My interest was in the names and numbers on the slabs of marble set into the ground.

"Why are there two numbers beside their names," I asked Baba.

"One is birth, the other is death," she said. "If you subtract the small number from the large one, you will see how old they were when they died."

We often walked along the waterfront and park area where wooden benches were strategically placed for people to sit on and rest. Each bench had plaques embedded into the wood with messages that started with *In Loving Memory of* – followed by a name of the deceased.

I spent many days walking around reading the plaques and counting off the numbers.

"Baba," I said. "I just subtracted the small number from the big one – this man was 82 when he died."

"Really?" Baba said. "You did the subtraction in your head?"

It seemed I did. Then I went to the next bench and again I got the correct age. And then something embarrassing happened. A lady sitting on a bench watched as I read off the numbers.

Baba said to her, "If you tell my grandson the year you were born, he'll tell you your age."

The lady looked at Baba as if to say *Really? He's just a kid.*

"Try it," Baba said. "Just give him the year."

The lady told me the number and when I subtracted it from the current year, I said "You are fifty-four."

"What?" she said, shaking her head. "How did you do that?"

I was around five years old back then.

Of course, when I got to high school and took calculus it was way much harder.

DIAPER SERVICE

"When I was 26 years old and my first baby – your Uncle Dee – was born," Baba said as she placed a huge package of diapers into our closet, "disposable diapers were not yet available. So instead of washing dirty diapers in the laundry room in the basement of the high-rise apartment building where we lived, we used a diaper service.

"Once a week, a truck with a picture of a stork holding a diaper in its beak, pulled up at the curb. The driver took away a pail of used soiled diapers, and left behind a stack of clean cotton ones, a clean pail and a disc of disinfectant.

"By the time your mother was born," she said, looking at me, "some genius invented the disposable diaper. With an absorbent liner and outside waterproof panties, there were no fears of leakage.

"Disposables were invented for the rich," Baba said. "But they did prevent baby rashes. When we went on a cottage vacation in Haliburton, your mother got so used to the dry feel of the disposables that when we came back home and went back to cotton diapers, she'd cry, 'I want my Pampers… I want my Pampers…'"

All the while Baba's telling us this, Mom is shaking her head. "Oh, really, Mother? You expect me to remember that?"

And then Mom brought out a picture she took of Baba washing my bum in the bathroom sink.

"Remember this?" Mom grinned at me.

"Really, Mother," I said, shaking my head. "You expect me to remember that?"

"One summer, when I was a kid," Baba said, "I had to take care of my nephew Peter, while his mother – my sister – went to work."

"One time, his diaper was so dirty I plunked one-year-old Peter inside the toilet bowl and kept flushing until the water thoroughly washed his behind. And all the time the kid is howling," Baba said laughing.

"When I regaled that bit to family and guests at a backyard barbeque to celebrate Peter's 50th birthday when I was still living in Ontario," she said, "it was the highlight of the day and an embarrassment for him."

"So," Peter said in rebuttal to Baba's idea of a ha-ha moment, "all those years of my fear of being flushed down the toilet is *your* fault?"

"I was 12 years old," Baba sparred with him. "What did you expect me to do? Let you run around with a dirty diaper? Think of it as a cold-wash bidet. Anyway, you survived just fine."

I was about to ask if she ever did that to me but then decided that was another one of those things I'd rather not know and definitely not even think about. It's just as well, for I cringe at the idea of being flushed down the toilet bowl.

QUESADILLAS COMING UP

Every once in a while, I'd luck out and go to a friend's house for a play day. And in return, at another time my friend would come over to spend the day at my house.

"Play Day?" Baba said. "What's with a Play Day? It's just another excuse for a kid's mother to pawn off her brat so she can have a day of peace. Free babysitting, that's what Play Day is."

"Yeah," I reminded her. "But when it's my turn to spend the full day with my friend at his house, I won't be around to bug you."

"Well, that makes all the difference in the world," she said. "In that case, I look forward to your next Play Day – away."

"Actually, it's our turn today, Baba. My friend Jason should be here any minute. Mom made the arrangements last night."

We lucked out on account of the sun was shining and no way did we want to stay indoors and be bossed around by Baba. So, off my friend and I went into the backyard and there we stayed, out of Baba's hair and away from my kid sister, who just started walking, so she wouldn't get in our way of playing.

"I'm making grilled cheese sandwiches for lunch," Baba announced. "Come inside and wash up."

"We don't want grilled cheese," I said. "My friend and I want cheese quesadillas."

"A what?" Baba said. "What are quesadillas made of?"

"Melted cheese on a pita." Jason, a vegetarian, gave Baba the ingredients of a simple quesadilla.

Baba made a weird scrunched up face. Twisting lower lip to one side, she rolled her eyes up to the ceiling. As if that's where she would find the answer to the riddle – what is the difference between a quesadilla and a grilled cheese sandwich?

"No pita," she said, checking the breadbasket and coming up empty. "But there's hoagie buns."

"Quesadilla is not made with hoagie buns." I reminded Baba.

"Really? When did you become a culinary connoisseur? Anyway, what's the difference? Buns are buns. They're all the same, made with the same flour."

So, Baba greased the bottoms of three halves of hoagie buns with butter and placed them into a large square grill pan.

"And, what do you want for lunch, little girl?" she said to Athena, who sat on the kitchen floor sucking her thumb. As if my one-year-old sister had a choice and if she could talk, she'd ask for something other than homemade baby food that Mom prepared.

Athena removed her thumb out of her mouth and raised her arms in the air. "Up, up," she announced. All she wanted was to be carried around by Baba.

"Sorry, kiddo," Baba said as she placed her into the high chair. "There's no way I can safely carry a 20-pound baby and work at the stove."

Baba cut several slices off a large chunk of cheddar cheese and layered them on the bottom part of the buns and covered them with the tops. With a large, flat lid she gently squished the buns, then flipped them over to melt the cheese and toast the other side.

Baba turned the cheese hoagies onto four round wooden boards and cut them in quarters.

"Voila," she announced with as much pride as if she just completed a piece of art and served us her version of a quesadilla.

My sister's wooden board held several tiny, bite size cubes in case she wanted to chew on them.

"You have to wait until they cool, kiddo," Baba cautioned and fed her from a bowl of what looked like mush – yet was probably a very tasty mixture of veggies and minced chicken or beef. "If you burn yourself, I don't want to have to blow into your mouth."

Jason and I gobbled our quesas.

"Is there any more?" I asked, munching on carrot sticks and apple slices.

"You want *more?*" Baba said, peering over her eyeglasses, just like that mean Mr. Bumble had said to *Oliver Twist*, in the book written by Charles Dickens.

A year or so later, Dad gave me a copy of *Oliver Twist* that his Dad gave him as a young boy. And over the next several years as it was read out loud to us, Baba always said *you want more?* that same way. Except she was a female version of that old grouch.

Two more buns went into the pan and Baba served us another portion of lunch.

"Actually, Baba," I said after all the crumbs were cleared off my board, "those were good quesadillas."

"Yea," said Jason, "not exactly like my Mom makes at home, but pretty good."

"Well," said Baba, "nothing ever tastes better than what your mom makes at home. But it's my first attempt at quesadillas – and without pita bread. Next time, I'll make you my favourite grilled cheese sandwiches. You'll love those even better."

I do believe Baba snickered, as she said that.

As time passed, I realized that Baba's grilled cheese sandwiches were almost identical to my version of quesadillas. Except for variety the cheese was white cheddar, instead of the yellow type. And the hoagie bun was replaced by slices of whole wheat bread or whatever she would pull out of the bread basket.

LET IT SNOW

We very rarely get any snow on the Sunshine Coast of British Columbia.

If we want to ski, we have two choices. For downhill skiing it's a two-hour drive along the paved Sea to Sky Highway to Whistler.

Or, for cross-country and tobogganing we need chains for our car tires to get up the unpaved logging road to Dakota Ridge. It's closer to home, but if chains were not used drivers who thought their all-weather tires were good enough up the snow-covered road, often swerved off and had to be pulled out of a ditch. My friend's Dad once took a chance and instead of enjoying the day up on the ski hill, a tow truck pulled us out of a deep snow bank and we headed back home. Next time, it was chains on.

Our first family trip to Dakota Ridge was awesome – lots of snow and sunny all day for great cross-country skiing. Even Baba went sliding down the road on a toboggan without falling off.

However, after spending the day in a shack heated only by a wood-burning stove while eating home-made sandwiches for lunch, she wasn't impressed.

"The area is great for snow and ski," Baba said, "but accommodations need huge improvements. And, if I win the lottery, I'll buy Dakota Ridge and turn it into a miniature Whistler with paved roads and decent après-ski chalets with restaurants. Just like my ski trips to the Laurentians, north of Montreal way back in the good old days when I lived in Quebec during the 1950s and '60s."

Quite often Baba dwelled on the past, but at her age memories of her good times was all she had.

Baba lived about a five-minute walk from her third-floor condo to our school. Behind our school was a park with a good slope of a hill, perfect for rolling down the soft green grass as we found out in the summers.

I was six and Athena three when the big snowfall started in December.

When Baba came to get me from school everything was a blanket of white. Even though we had no toboggan or proper winter clothing, many kids ran towards the snow-covered hill.

"Just go down once or twice," Baba yelled at me as I ran in their direction. "You'll get sick if you get too wet."

When my sister followed me, Baba ran to her parked car and came back with two plastic bags. She then shoved Athena's legs through the handles of a grocery bag.

"At least your toosh, your bum, won't get soaked," Baba mumbled as she fumbled with the plastic bag to secure it around her waist just like a diaper.

It was Athena's first time on snow and she didn't seem to care if anyone saw her make-shift waterproof pants.

She slid on her bum – weeeeeeeing with delight and with arms in the air, no control whatsoever where she was going, she spun around as she headed downhill. With absolutely no fear, she experienced sliding on snow for the first time. And when she came to a stop at the bottom of the hill, she yelled *again* and scrambled up the slippery slope to the top. And again, plunked herself on the ground and down she went.

The slide down took three to four seconds, so running back up was easy and quick.

Up the hill we trudged and down the hill we slid. All the while Baba stood by watching us and snapped her small digital camera, which she always kept in a tote bag.

After about ten or so trips up and down, she decided we had enough. Reluctantly, we walked up to her apartment and quickly removed our soaked clothes and into the tub of hot water we went to warm our bodies. And rid ourselves of possibly catching a cold – or worse.

"You should have let me put a plastic bag on you, too," Baba said as she wrung out my snow-soaked pants and underwear into the bathroom sink.

No way would I be seen caught by some school mate who would spread the word next day that I wore a Baba-made diaper sliding down the snow hill.

Baba always had plenty of clothes at her place that she bought on sale for us. So on went dry clothes, followed by cups of hot chocolate. We experienced our first snow outing. Just like at a ski lodge, Baba said.

Next day, when she came to get me at the school, she held a huge round plastic disc in her hand and my sister was dressed in a snowsuit, hat and winter mitts. And Baba made me put on snow pants that she managed to buy at the Thrift Store that morning. This time we ran up the hill and slid down as much as we wanted without getting soaked.

Normally, we on the Sunshine Coast would be lucky to get a few flakes a year. But that year, it snowed and snowed, and days later it was still snowing.

Schools were shut down for over two weeks during Christmas and New Year. Yet, daily, that hill was filled with kids tobogganing.

Baba often told us stories of driving and skiing in Ontario where winters were sometimes brutal with lots of snowstorms.

"There was no such thing as stay-at-home snow days when I was a kid," she said. "No special buses to pick us up. Walking was the only way to get to school – rain or snow was never an excuse for missing classes."

One evening when Baba drove home from our place, her small 4-cylinder car got stuck on the snow-covered road.

"I'm in the middle of the road, my wheels are spinning – I smell the burning rubber and I'm going nowhere," she told us later.

"Why didn't you walk back to our place and get me?" Dad said.

"Do you have a plough in your backyard? You couldn't help, anyway. There were several inches of snow on all the roads," she said. "I managed to pull into somebody's driveway and abandoned the car there. Of course, by the time I walked home there was a message on my telephone answering machine.

"The tow truck came by to get me with my car keys. A few minutes later the car was back on the road, the tow truck following me. Finally inch by inch, I made it home. And as I turned off the ignition and said a huge prayer to God for bringing me home safely, the driver handed me a ticket for a $60 towing charge.

"I was so pissed – oops, sorry kiddos, didn't mean to use a bad word – I mailed a letter and a copy of the towing receipt to the Mayor's office. But, of course, I was never reimbursed."

"What's 'reimbursed'?" Athena took her thumb out of her mouth long enough to ask and then back in it went as she stared at Baba and waited for an answer.

"'Reimbursed', little girl, means pay back. I had to pay the towing company for their truck to pull my car out when I got stuck in the snow because the roads weren't ploughed. Never even heard from those in charge of road clearing with an apology as to why they didn't send out snow trucks – which this *little rinky-dink* town has probably *none* because it hardly ever snows here – to clear the roads."

That winter was a fluke. The next decent snowfall we had I was 13 – seven years later.

But I lucked in, as my parents enrolled me in a Biathlon Ski Club in Whistler and for the next several years I enjoyed training in cross-country skiing every weekend from fall to spring.

HOWL AT THE MOON

"Howling at the moon connects you with things that one cannot touch," Baba said.

I had no idea what that meant, but shortly after we learned about her philosophy of gazing up into the sky. During a full moon.

We're in the car – it's dark out. Baba's driving us home after spending some time at her apartment watching television. On account of we don't have cable and she does. On account of we have a life and she doesn't. Except for us, she said, we are all the life she has and needs – and basic cable.

Baba drove the car onto a parking lot of a small shopping area with a few stores that had closed for the night.

"Come on," she said, un-strapping Athena out of her seat. "Get out of the car."

I obeyed and we're standing in the dark leaning against the front of the car with its headlights on.

"Look up!" she ordered us to stare up at the dark sky.

High above was one of the biggest balls I've ever seen. Its bright light illuminated the whole sky and in the shadows stand silhouettes of tall, dark trees, waving gently back and forth in the light breeze.

"It's picture perfect," she said. "I wish I had a camera that took decent photos at night."

We stared at the moon, admiring its brilliance and then the weirdest sound came out of Baba.

'Wooooooooooooo!"

Baba's bonkers, she's gone off her rocker.

"Baba, what are you doing?" I asked.

"I'm howling at the moon, kid," she said. "Try it. It's amazing to be able to howl. Only happens at full moon. Once a month."

I looked around – there were no people within sight to possibly report us for creating a disturbance. So, I gave it a try.

"Hooooowwwwllll." I let out a guttural sound as loud as I could.

Athena is right in there with Baba. Woooooo... Woooooo... Woooo... The two of them staring at the sky and making enough noise to wake up the whole neighbourhood. Or attract coyotes that have been known to roam our woods and streets. Or, yikes, a bear!

Next thing we know, a police cruiser with no siren but lights flashing, parked alongside our car.

"Oh, oh, there's gonna be trouble," my sister said. When she first discovered she liked that phrase, she got into the habit of often using it whenever she felt she should warn us of impending trouble or danger.

"Is everything okay?" the policeman said, as he walked towards us, tapping his hip with his hand. I guess there was a baton there, or a gun!

"Everything's fine, Officer," Baba said. Leaning towards him, she whispered something that only he could hear.

The policeman looked up into the sky and chuckled.

"Have a great night, kids," he said, got back into his car and drove away.

"Did you tell him we were howling at the moon?" I said.

"Yep."

"Lucky we didn't get arrested," I said.

"No law against staring into the sky," Baba said, and she snapped my sister into her car seat, the two of them gave off another long and loud wooooo.

"Why have I not seen such a moon before?" I asked, as we drove home.

"Because it only comes at night – and most of the time, you're already asleep."

"Do it again, Baba," Athena said. My sister always wanted to re-do things that made her laugh.

"Next full moon, kiddo," Baba said.

I went to sleep that night wondering whether Baba was sane or did she really go off her rocker during the full moon, as the legend goes. For I had no idea what she did after she dropped us off at our home. For all I know, she went back to that same spot for another howling. I've read stories of wolves howling at the moon, but never a grandmother. This was possibly a first.

The next morning at breakfast, Athena let out a loud howl. When I told my parents how we almost got arrested last night, they just kept on eating their breakfast. I had hoped they would finally put Baba into an old age funny farm and get us a decent and much younger nanny.

"Anyone hurt?" Mom asked, as she swallowed a mouthful of Cheerios.

I guess if neither one of us was hurt in any way, it was an issue not worthy of further discussion.

"You know," Mom said. "Other than family visits, I never saw my Ukrainian grandmother do anything out of the ordinary."

"Yeah," I said. "You were pretty lucky you didn't have to do all those weird things that Baba makes us do with her."

The look on Mom's face said that maybe she might have missed out on bits of life with her Baba – that she only saw once or twice a year.

And, maybe one day I may be grateful for the experience. Weird as it was. But at that time, I hoped I'd grow up real fast so never again would I have to stare at the dark sky, and howl at the moon with an old lady.

BABA'S TALE
– UKRAINE –
1944

MY FAMILY

The eldest of Papa's five daughters was Anastazia, 20. Next came Elizabeth at 18, Maria at 16, Petro 14, twin boys who died at birth, Anna at eight. And me, Papa's favourite. So he said whenever I asked which of us he loved best.

"After God," Papa said. "I love you most."

"Why do you love God more than me?" I didn't understand who or what God was. How can Papa love somebody who never came to visit us? I never heard God talking back to Papa. I had often heard Papa talk to God. Sometimes he even got mad at God and then prayed for His forgiveness. It was a moment of disappointment, Papa said, that made him angry with God and if he felt he was forgiven, he promised he would never think bad thoughts of God again.

But there were times Papa must have forgotten his promise and spoke to God in an angry way.

"What good is hail to me, dear God, I ask you?" Papa spoke to the sky. "Rain I could use. Hail? Hail is useless! It destroyed Olena's tomatoes. Send out the sun and melt that hail and give us a nice spring shower."

Other times Papa blamed God for things he could not fix himself, like after the crows ate half of the cucumber and sunflower seeds in the garden.

"Keep those pesky birds away from my crops!" Papa yelled up at the sky. "One of these days I'll take a shotgun to them!"

And whenever I asked Papa how does he know that God hears our prayers, Papa assured me that He does. He sees and knows everything. Every minute of the day. God does.

"In the whole world, Papa? At the same time?"

"Yes, my little one. All at the same time."

"How can that be?"

Was God there when Nicholas and Taras died? Why did He let it happen? But that time Papa was not angry at God, as he was sad. No matter how hard he prayed, Nicholas and Taras never woke up.

"Why must we love God more than ourselves?" I needed to know.

"Because my little one, we must thank God for all the good he has done for us. It takes very little to love God. He's not demanding like some children are," Papa said with a smile. "And God does not ask so many silly questions like you do."

"Then you love me more than you love Mama, don't you Papa?"

"Yes, I do," he said winking at Mama. Quite often she and I fought for Papa's affection. In the end, somehow or other we both won. Or so it seemed.

Papa called me his little angel. But the rest of the family said the black sheep of the family suited me best. Except for my mother, who just hugged me, as she didn't want to take the blame for my birth.

I, too, almost died at birth. I was born in mid-December, 1939. Maybe I even caused the war – my sisters said years later, as if needing to blame someone, a child, for the horror we would endure.

Mama had been tending to a newborn calf in the barn when I decided I had enough of swimming around in water. It was time for me to make my entry into the world. Poor Mama buckled under with such excruciating pain, that she laid down right there on the ground, in the *hay. No way was she in any shape to walk the fifty metres from the barn to the house. Fortunately, the next time I again decided to leave her womb, Mama screeched loud enough for Maria to come to her aid.*

With the winter, there were no fields to tend, so Papa worked in town for a furniture manufacturer. By the time Papa came home in the evening, there I was all bundled up and asleep. As soon as Papa saw me, he looked at Mama and said, "No more!"

And crossed himself. Three times.

ANASTAZIA

The eldest of my siblings, Anastazia, was more like a second mother to me.

During the week, Anastazia worked as a finisher for a tailor in town. A lover of detail, Anastazia ensured that each suit sold to the well-to-do was expertly finished.

A few months after Anastazia's husband joined the Ukrainian army and went off to fight the war, baby Ostap was born. Anastazia loved to embroider fine linens with colourful threads in cross stitch patterns. But kerosene lamps quickly tired the eyes.

So, while most of us went off to the market on Saturdays, Anastazia spent the daylight hours working on a blouse, or dress, with her baby son cooing beside her on a blanket or in an oak cradle that Papa crafted.

ELIZABETH

Elizabeth and Maria could have passed for twins. Except they were born two years apart. Elizabeth was not quite two when Mama gave birth to Maria. Right from the start the resemblance was obvious. They both had the same mousey brown unruly hair that, unless it was braided, flew all over in the wind. Each had bright blue eyes, with a short curled up stubby nose and high cheek bones, with one deep dimple. Elizabeth's dimple was on her right cheek and Maria's on the left. So when they stood with faces scrunched together side by side, they looked like one big distorted face with dimples on either the inside or the outside. But that's where the similarities ended.

Elizabeth was tall and slim, with long strong legs and loved to dance through the meadows.

"There is no such thing as female Cossacks," Petro told Elizabeth when she spoke of joining the forces to protect our homeland.

"Well, there should be! And one day I'll appoint myself their leader and rid Ukraine of all those Russian Bolsheviks! Independence day will come, just wait and see."

Little did Elizabeth know that within a very short time, she would be given that chance.

But would she succeed in her quest for freedom? No one could predict the future.

MARIA

Maria was the gypsy in the family with an uncanny ability to predict the future. Well, somewhat. But when World War II broke out, her insights into world events became more and more believable.

Maria enjoyed her trips to the market in the city. A gathering place for all walks of life – both poor and rich. But Maria mainly admired the rich. Especially the young men, who dressed in crisp cotton shirts and pressed pants. Not like the boys on the farms who wore the same clothes in the fields, day after day.

Maria vowed that no hands of a farm boy would ever touch her.

Not with dirt under their fingernails. A life of culture was her dream. She was not quite good enough to be a concert violinist, but Papa's eyes always teared up when Maria played the violin.

"One day I'll meet that rich man who will take me away from this farm and all this dirt. If I want to work in the fields for the rest of my life, I'd marry Yuri. But I don't and I won't. Growing old on a farm is not for me. I don't want my lovely hands roughened by calluses. Farm work is for peasants. I want to travel the world, go to America. My rich husband will lavish me with such gifts, you can't even imagine the riches," she told us.

Farm life was definitely not for her. So every Saturday Maria set off to the market in search of a rich husband.

But before Maria reached her sixteenth birthday, fate changed her plans so drastically that even she looked at those poor farm boys in a different light.

PETRO

After the twin boys were buried, Petro and Papa became the only males in the household. The two males had six females to boss them around.

When Petro wasn't in school, he helped Papa work the fields.

At 14, Petro already stood a head taller than Papa. A strapping young man, he dreamed of a life as an army officer.

When men were being recruited into the Ukrainian Army, Petro begged Papa to allow him to enlist.

"Are you crazy?" Papa objected. "You want to get yourself shot? Anyway, I need you to work the farm."

"But Papa, we must protect our Ukraine. The Russians are killing us and taking our land away."

"Protect, yes. But to commit suicide? No! Never! You're just a child."

"But I want to be like the Cossacks. Rid Ukraine of all those Bolsheviks!"

"Cossacks? You heard too many stories about the Cossacks. Riding around the countryside on a horse with a sabre is not as colourful as you might think. That's no life for a boy your age."

"What if I'm called to duty, Papa? Then, will you let me go?"

"Then, you will have to go. Even I will not be able to stop you. Heaven forbid that day should come," Papa said, crossing himself.

Papa sure crossed himself a lot.

ANNA

Anna loved food. And she looked it. The last one from the table, she never turned down a second helping of potatoes, corn mamalega or meat of any kind. By the time Anna was nine, she had enough fat on her to make another girl about half her size. No matter how hard Mama tried to keep her from overeating, Anna always sneaked food from the pantry and shoved it down her throat.

It didn't help either that Anna was lazy. Very lazy. Her daily chores of cleaning up the kitchen after meals were never done. Instead of putting leftover food away for another meal, as she was told to do, she ate it instead. Too tired to clean up, she'd go outside and sit under an apple or pear tree and rest. As if she had just finished her share of chores and deserved a much-needed rest. By the time Mama came in from working in the field, it was late afternoon and Anna had awoken from her nap. Anna believed she fooled Mama into thinking she'd done her chores. And often, Elizabeth or Maria complained about Anna's laziness and they had to clean up after her.

"Tomorrow," Mama urged, waving her finger at Anna. "Tomorrow you do your chores or you don't come to town with us on Saturday."

Anna could not imagine us going to town without her. Dutifully she'd tend to the chores, but her good deeds would only last a day or two. And then she was back to her old lazy ways again, eating more than her share.

But it didn't take too long for Anna to lose all that extra weight. For once we set out to escape the Communists, hearty meals of roasted potatoes, oozing with butter, were soon a faded memory of plentiful harvests back in our homeland. And a second helping of egg-infused babka, well, that was a dream she learned soon enough to accept as just that – a dream.

EAT CABBAGE & POOP ALL DAY

Every Tuesday, Thursday and Saturday, Baba ruled our lives. Three days a week, like it or not, she cooked for us and made sure we had a proper upbringing according to *Baba's Rule Book of Life*.

When it came to eating vegetables, I was reluctant to try any that Baba put in front of me. Although I ate cucumbers, carrots and sometimes yellow peppers, celery was not what I looked forward to unless she cut it into bite size pieces topped with peanut butter. When I gagged at the idea of eating peas, she told us how she once tried to bribe our mother that she would give her a million dollars if she ate one single green pea.

I guess it didn't work. On account of Mom is not a millionaire and, like most people we know, has to work for a living.

Baba tried to brainwash us into believing that a regular dosage of green cabbage, made our poop regular. Oh, goody.

Of course, I refused to come anywhere near that stinky vegetable. There have been times during the three days a week she cooked our meals I'm sure she somehow managed to include tiny bits of chopped up green cabbage into our soups or even its broth. Because whenever we ate soup that Baba cooked, we had no problem pooping.

Once a month or so, Baba had a desire for *real* fish 'n chips. Not the store-bought frozen stuff.

"That's not even real fish that I fed my kids – your mother – years ago and didn't realize that it was just bits of fish mixed in with flour and bread crumbs to bind them together into sticks with zero food value – just useless fillers."

So, we'd drive out of town to a little place in Roberts Creek called Sharkey's Fish and Chips, a take-out shop tucked away off the highway in a clearing of trees, where they cooked with fresh fish – sometimes caught the same day of frying, or so they advertised.

It was not licensed as a restaurant, Baba said – no tables and chairs to sit on to eat our lunch. And she definitely did not want to stink up her car with fish and possibly dirty her upholstery with ketchup.

We drove down the highway a bit and turned up a long, unpaved, pot-holed road that led into Cliff Gilker Park. Dad and Mom often took me there for long hikes along a trail that goes on for miles. Or metres, if you're thinking in metric. We also played many soccer games in the field.

The first time we went there to eat our crispy fish and fries for lunch, we were about to sit at a wooden picnic table covered with bird droppings.

"Wait!" Baba yelled, and took a roll out of the car and with wads of paper towels cleaned it up and then lined the table with more towels. As she's doing this, she's trying not to gag.

Finally we're settled and as I squeeze ketchup out of a packet onto the fries, I notice Baba munching some sort of concoction out of a small paper container.

"What's that?" I asked.

"Coleslaw," she said. "Want some?"

"What's it made of?"

"Carrots, maybe little celery... and cabbage."

"Gross!" I said at the word cabbage. "You'll never get me to eat it!"

"I'll give you five dollars if you try one forkful," she said with a look that said I'd be foolish not to jump at her generous offer.

"Five dollars? Wow? I'm not even old enough to go to the store by myself, so what was I going to do with all that money?"

"You can save it to buy Mommy a flower for Mother's Day," she said.

I knew she was bribing me, but….

"Okay, I'll try one mouthful. And if it taste gross, I'm spitting it right out! So be prepared, Baba! I'll eat it – but I won't like it!"

"Okay, but you gotta give it a few good chews before you make up you mind. Let the juices rest on your tongue so you get the real taste of all the ingredients."

As she raised a fork with bits of cabbage towards my mouth, I closed my eyes, felt it on my tongue and told myself not to think about the weird smell… just eat it… I gave it a slight chew… oh no… gag… chew... hmmm... not bad... with a tinge of vinegar, it kinda tasted like pickles, which I loved… chew… swallow.

Baba's grinning at me, "Good stuff, eh?"

No comment from me, I was still trying to gather enough saliva in my mouth to rinse away the cabbage taste and swallow it all in one big gulp. I grabbed my soda and took a long drink to wash away the cabbage taste.

"You're lucky, kid," Baba said with a wide grin. "That I will **never** make you eat turnips."

"Really? Why not?"

I vaguely remember Mom mashing up potatoes with another cream-coloured root vegetable. Even though the potato tasted okay there was still a slight odd yet strong tinge when I took a mouthful. I guess that was turnip Mom tried to make us eat by hiding it.

"Because we lived on turnips during and after the war – rotten or not – it all got eaten. Or you starved. Maybe I'll tell you that story another time," Baba said, dismissing the issue.

"So?" she said taking another forkful. "Good coleslaw, eh?"

"It's okay," I said after I realized that mixing cabbage with a dressing made it okay to eat. "So, where's my five dollars?"

"I just spent all my money on our lunch. Don't worry, kiddo, I'm good for it."

"So, how much will you give me if I eat another mouthful of coleslaw?" I said. Maybe this bribery could be a lucrative money-maker.

"Nothing," she said with a know-it-all smirk. "I just gave you a great gift. And the next time you poop, you'll thank me."

AWARDS

Never, never, let your Grandmother know that you won an award. Of any kind. Not even a mere recognition of a colourful ribbon.

However, if there's a guarantee of money, then brag all you want.

If it's a 1st place red ribbon, I was rewarded a toonie – a coin worth two dollars in Canada. And a 2nd place blue, a loonie – a one dollar coin.

"You earned it, kiddo," Baba said, grinning ear to ear as she handed me a bunch of coins that she dug out of her purse.

"Don't tell your mother," she whispered in my ear and tucked the money into my hand. "Put it in your piggy bank. Save it for when you get older, so you can buy yourself something nice."

I was five years old, the first time I played T-ball in little league. There was no pitcher hurling the ball at the batter. The object was to hit the ball that the catcher placed on top of a thick stick in the ground in front of home plate.

My first time up, I stood ready, feet apart, tightly gripped the bat and just as I was about to hit the ball, I closed my eyes and as I swung I spun right around. When I gained my balance and opened my eyes, the ball had not even moved. To make matters worse, some of the kids on the sidelines were laughing. Really loud.

It was horrible to hear my teammates mocking me. But when the next kid at bat also missed the ball, I found myself giggling along with the rest of the team.

I soon learned how to hit the ball and run bases and when absolutely necessary to save the game, I'd slide home to ensure I was safe instead of being tagged out – even though Baba warned me of the hazards of gravel embedded in the skin of my legs or behind.

That first year, every kid on my team got a trophy for winning a tournament and coming first in the league.

Also, that season I got the Sportsmanship Medal, because the coaches voted me *a nice guy.*

When I'm not at bat, I root for the guy that is, urging him to hit the ball or run to the next base before the opponents tag him out.

"Why are you rooting for the other team?" Baba asked me after my first game.

"I'm rooting for my friend."

"But he's on the opposing team."

"But he's my best friend."

I didn't understand what the big deal was. What difference did it make who you root for? We're trained to whack the ball with the bat and when the ball flies through the air, we run like hell around the diamond, and make sure to touch each base! And if your legs can't carry you fast enough, slide to home. But don't hurt yourself.

Baba sure confused me. First she tells me to play nice and treat other kids as I would want to be treated by them and then she reminds me that the object of the game is to beat the opponent and be victorious.

Make up your mind, Baba.

When I turned ten, I qualified to take the worldwide Fibonacci Math Test. At the last day of my grade five, students and parents sat in the school gym as teachers presented various academic and athletic awards.

Next thing I knew, my name was called. I ran up to the front and as the teacher placed a ribbon around my neck with a medal hanging from it everyone started clapping and amidst all noise I heard a loud voice, "Proud of you, kiddo!" Only one person had the nerve to embarrass me that way.

After I won the Fibonacci Math Medal, the whole world knew it. Baba blinded me snapping her camera to capture how proud a kid looked with a round piece of metal attached to a ribbon hung around his neck.

Anyone she *Liked* on her FaceBook page was notified. If a reply came back with *congrats,* or *so proud of you,* Baba would share it again and again and again. Until it seemed the whole world was sending me words of encouragements.

"Look," she'd point at the screen of her laptop. "Look at the people who love you."

Really, Baba? Even she had no idea who 99% of these people were. But she was in her glory that the whole world knew that her only grandson was "a math genius". Her words – definitely not mine.

"So," Baba said while we celebrated and munched on sushi in the local Japanese restaurant. "You should be very proud of yourself, kiddo."

"I am," I said, still not believing I achieved such an honour.

"You know," Baba said. "I think you're the smartest kid in the whole school in math".

"No, I'm not. There are other kids smarter than me."

"Sure, okay, but how many kids in grade five got the Fibonacci award?"

"One."

"And how many kids are there in your school that were eligible?"

"I don't know exactly how many, maybe 30 or 40."

"So," Baba said pointing her finger into the air, "out of 40 kids, only one won the award."

"Yeah, Baba. That's how it works... bunch of students apply, and only one wins."

"And what kid won?" She peered into my face as if accusing me of some wrongdoing.

"Errr..." I managed. "I did."

And finally as if she was some lawyer in a courtroom drama, she flung her arm in the air and announced, "I rest my case."

One year, I entered a track and field event for 50-metre dash. I won, and when I showed Baba my 1ˢᵗ place ribbon and certificate, she hugged me so hard I almost farted.

"Tell me all about the race," she said.

So, I'm at the starting line. Bent down, hands just this side of the white chalk, one foot solid on the ground, the other heel raised, ready to sprint. At the sound of the starter pistol, I took off, pacing myself, hoping no one would ever catch up to me. Forty metres to go. One leg over the other, with each step I cover a few inches of gravel as I make my way to the finish line. And then just as in *Chariots of Fire* the music starts in my head, ta. ta. ta. ta. ta. ta...... I knew the piece because when Baba found out I was going to run, she made me watch the ending of the movie. The music was pretty impressive and, as I made my way to the finish line, I lifted my arms in the air and broke through the ribbon. Just like the runners do in the Olympics.

When I finally told Baba the reason I got first place was because I was one of only two kids registered for the race and the other runner unfortunately, or maybe fortunate for me, left early on account of there was a huge rainfall at the start of the competition. So, I was the only competitor. I raced against myself. And I won. By default.

Okay, so I won without having to worry about the competition. Actually I had set a record, albeit a personal one.

As I advanced in track, I trained hard to better my best.

Over the years that followed whenever I told Baba I entered a race, she never let me forget my first triumph of being the sole runner and with a grin she'd ask, "And how many runners were there in *that* race?"

CLOUDS

"Look up!" Baba yelled, as she parked her car in our driveway.

"It's a camel!" She pointed toward the sky. The light blue sky is filled with clouds. Huge, fluffy ones with various shapes and tinges of white and grey.

"Too fat to be a camel," I said as I followed her lead and scanned the sky above.

"Maybe it just filled itself with water for the long journey across the desert," she said.

"Desert?" said Athena. "What's a desert?"

Athena finally learned to talk, forming a few words together and drove me crazy asking many, many questions about everything she didn't quite understand.

We got out of the car and followed Baba to an open area alongside our townhouse complex. A grassy common area that my friends and I often used as a playground.

Baba sat down on the grass and told us to do the same. She lay back on the ground and stared into the sky. My sister is right there with her, following the leader. The two of them are ooo-ing and aaa-ing at the sights above.

"Watch," she said, "just watch those clouds as they move ever so slowly and change shapes."

So, I sat down there with them and before I knew it I'm also playing their game.

"It's an elephant." I pointed to a clump of dark grey clouds. "Wait, wait, it's changing into a rhinoceros."

"Looks like a mother duck and her babies," Baba said, and as the clouds moved along she changed her mind. "Oh no, one ducky just fell out of the sky."

"Snake," my sister said and got to her feet. She pointed to a long tiny creature slithering along the grass.

"Whaaaaat?" Baba screamed, jumping to her feet. She freaked out as it rapidly disappeared into a clump of bushes.

Baba had a fear of anything that crawled along the ground. Bugs and spiders are okay, she often said, because they had legs.

From then on whenever we played in that area, she always brought a huge blanket for us to lie on and a chaise chair for her to sit in.

The next time I gazed into the sky and watched as huge clouds crept along, I asked if we could lie down and play the guessing game again. But it was late fall and the grass was not warm or dry enough, so Baba hoisted Athena onto the hood of her car and laid her on her back to gaze into the sky above.

"Get up here." She motioned me to climb up.

"Dad would never let us do that with his Toyota," I said. "What if we scratch your car?"

"Then don't scratch my car," she said, shrugging her shoulders.

I guess our game-playing was more important to her than a possible scratch on her 10-year old Hyundai Accent that had been driven across Canada and had definitely – just like she, herself – had seen better days.

BABA AND WINE

"Drinking wine is like eating grapes," said Baba, "but in the liquid form."

The first time we went with her to buy wine, even before we took one step through the automatic doors of the liquor store, she rhymed off the rules.

"Don't swing your hands... don't touch any bottles... don't run... don't skip... or turn... or spin. Do not move – just wait here until I get back."

My sister and I both stood in a corner at the front door, away from any aisles. In no time at all, Baba was at the cash register with her wine and out we went. Then she proceeded to tell us how proud she was, that we are so mindful and didn't break any bottles by running through the store, like those other bad-mannered kids do.

The only time we were allowed to walk through the store was when we returned bottles and beer cans for refund.

And each time she repeated her rules, and at times ended with, "You break any bottle and guess what? Your dad pays for it. Not me. And he will not be happy. Got it?"

Yeah, yeah, Baba, we got it. It was the same ritual, over and over.

After several of these trips, I asked why she didn't go to the liquor store on her days off when she's not sitting us – instead of schlepping us everywhere to do her own shopping.

To this she replied, "You need exposure, kiddo. If children

71

are not taught how to behave outside their home, they grow up without any manners. And run amok in public places."

Once, Baba hoisted a 4-litre box of red domestic wine onto the counter and said to the cashier, "Tell me one more time, why is wine good for me?"

In reply, the man said, "I don't really know, but for sure it's got a whole lot less sugar than soda pop."

"Good answer." Baba smiled gratefully at the man who gave her one more reason to keep on enjoying wine.

Later, she told us that during World War II soldiers used the dark cola to polish their brass buttons of their uniforms before trudging off to battle. So, whenever we asked for a treat of a soda, she'd always say, "Do you want the inside of your stomach as shiny as a brass button?"

From time to time, Baba gathered all the refundables on our balcony and off we went to get our deposits back.

One time, with plastic bags full of empty beer cans in hand, my sister and I walked through the automatic door and proceeded towards the bottle return section at back. Baba was lagging behind and before she caught up to us, we were way ahead.

"Hey," a store worker stopped us, "you can't come in here."

The clerk must have thought we were waif kids returning found bottles for coins, until he saw Baba and then let us through.

The only good thing about going with Baba to recycle bottles is she always gave us a couple quarters each and we ran through the mall to get bubble gum or a handful of Smarties from candy dispensing machines.

"When I lived in Ontario, I once made my own wine at the do-it-yourself wine place," Baba said. "I had 24 bottles in my storage room and one night I was awoken by a huge *pop*. It sounded like a gunshot or a car backfiring coming from outside, so I ignored it. Next morning, there was wine all over the floor from one bottle that had not sealed properly. Lucky for me, it was white wine – had it been red, what a mess it would have been."

"Yeah, Baba," I said, "you're better off letting the pros make your wine."

"Yeah, and I can do what I do best," she said with a wink. "Just drink it."

DANIEL O'DONNELL

"Guess where I'm going?" Baba announced one day.

Home, I had hoped she would say, but when I did not question her she added, "Daniel O'Donnell is performing at the Orpheum Theatre in Vancouver."

Are you kidding me, I wanted to say. Ever since she introduced me to his music, I've been a great fan. She bought CDs of *all* his greatest hits and blasted them non-stop in her car wherever we went. But no way would I expect her to take me along. Especially an overnight stay in Vancouver.

So I said "So what?"

"So, I got two tickets, top balcony. Want to come with me?" she asked. "We can make it a special event, just you and me. We'll stay overnight at a hotel, maybe explore some sights."

"Me?" I said. "You want me to go with you?" And yet, I didn't know if seeing Daniel O'Donnell in person was worth being subjected to Baba's orders for two whole days.

"My birthday gift to you, kiddo," she said. "It's so expensive this may last you for the next few years."

"Okay, but only if Mom and Dad will let me."

"Of course they'll let you," she said. "I checked with them first before I bought the tickets. I wouldn't waste several months of my wine budget on a ticket for you if you couldn't go."

When I bragged about going to a Daniel O'Donnell concert to the office secretary at our school, she said she knew someone who worked behind the scenes at the Orpheum Theatre. A couple of weeks later, I get an envelope in the mail *all the way from Ireland*. An autographed publicity photo of Daniel and a note saying he looked forward to meeting me at his concert.

I know Baba was just as excited as I was and when the big day came, off we went on the ferry to Vancouver. My parents checked us into a hotel and left Baba and me to enjoy our adventure.

Actually, it was fun. Baba's totally different in demeanour when she's not in charge of us kids. We were like two people on vacation. I must admit I did not act ornery or disagreeable every time she asked me to do something.

But I knew I had to behave, on account Mom and Dad were not there to bail me out. If I didn't, she might leave me stranded in the city. Nah, she wouldn't do that, would she? Well, I wasn't about to test it out, so I decided to act like a normal person. How, she often said, we should behave.

We toured downtown Vancouver, had sushi for lunch, watched construction of a subway system being built and even went to a huge jewellery store. Why? We just happened to pass by it and Baba said it was like going to Tiffany's – a very expensive store, with lush carpets on stairs going up to the second floor. At the bottom of the staircase stood a man, dressed in a dark business suit with matching tie and crisp white shirt.

"Welcome to our store," he greeted us as if we were somebody special.

Baba ooohed and aaahed as we walked around the glass display cases with gold and silver and diamonds gleaming – all beckoning customers to "buy me, buy me".

"Look, they're making a movie," Baba said as we walked towards a side street that was partitioned off for a group of people, camera equipment and tons of cables.

She then snapped her camera as I stood by a police car with a New York license plate.

Back at the hotel, we showered and changed into evening clothes. I would have been just as comfortable in my shorts and tee, but Baba insisted.

"We must look presentable," she said. "In case we get to meet Daniel. You wouldn't want him to think we Canadians are bums, would you?"

Baba wore a long black skirt with a white lace top. Can't go wrong with traditional colours, she said.

My clothes were all brand new: beige pants, a proper buttoned-down, long-sleeved, white shirt and an argyle knit vest. I even wore a new pair of decent suede shoes.

We had dinner at a fancy restaurant with white tablecloths and matching napkins. We shared a double order of fish 'n chips and a Caesar salad. Baba had a glass of red wine and I had a real treat – Coca Cola. For dessert it was chocolate ice cream sundae with biscuits and Baba had her favourite, apple pie with a slice of cheddar cheese on top.

Finally, we're off to the theatre by taxi.

Daniel is a real showman. He sang all our favourites, just like the songs on CDs in Baba's car.

At intermission, we went into the foyer to mingle with the audience. I had a glass of juice and Baba sipped a glass of red wine.

"I'm not driving tonight, so why not treat myself," she said, as if she needed an excuse and ran it by me for approval.

When we returned to our seats, the lights were all turned on and Daniel sat on the stage and read a few letters that he received from his fans. And then the most awesome thing happened.

He said he wanted to meet his youngest fan – a six-year-old from the Sunshine Coast. I thought nothing of it, until he called out *my name*! So excited, I jumped up and ran to the railing and looking down from the balcony I frantically waved at him, "I'm here! I'm here!"

Daniel looked up and waved back and said he wanted me to be first in line for his *meet and greet* event.

After the show, Baba and I were ushered like some famous movie stars to the front of the long line, while all the fans just stood by grinning at us.

Daniel approached us, bent down on his knee and looked me straight in the eyes. I don't remember all he said and neither did Baba when I asked her later, because she was too busy snapping her camera. I do remember Daniel telling me he liked my vest and tie and thanked us for coming to his concert.

I heard Baba sniff a couple of times, maybe so she wouldn't cry. Geez, some people are so emotional.

"We got the royal treatment," Baba boasted while describing the event to my parents at dinner the next day.

A few days later, Baba handed me a small photo album of our adventure.

There were several photos of me just walking along the streets of Vancouver and my first time without parents on the ferry to home as a walk-on.

And the best – three photos of Daniel and I, that will always be my favourites of my first big night on the town.

There was one shot of me sleeping in the hotel room bed with only my head on the pillow, eyes shut, visible. Hmm, I don't remember her taking that one.

"So, where are you taking me for my next birthday," I asked Baba while Mom and Dad looked at the photos and hopefully were comforted that their precious kid survived two days in the big City without them.

"Nowhere, kid," she said. "This trip ate up my budget for your next ten birthdays."

Darn.

"However, if Bobby Darin was still alive," Baba said, "we'd definitely go to his concert."

"Who's Bobby Darin?"

"You never heard of Bobby Darin?" she looked at me as if I were from another planet. And then proceeded to dance the Twist and sing, "Splish, splash, I was taking a bath..."

And so, Baba introduced me to the music of her youth – the wonderful '50s and '60s.

Her world – not mine.

BOBBY DARIN

"Look what I bought for you," Baba said and plunked a DVD into her television. *"Beyond the Sea,* a movie about Bobby Darin, starring Kevin Spacey."

Actually, Baba got two copies of the movie, one for us to watch at our house and the other for her place.

For the next year or so, we almost wore the DVD out. I knew every word of every song on it.

But the real treat, not so much for me, but for Baba, was *Come September.* A movie with Rock Hudson, Gina Lollobrigida and Sandra Dee. And introducing a young actor, Bobby Darin, singing and dancing to his big hit, "Multiplication… that's the name of the game…."

Next time we saw Baba, she handed me a black disk, about six inches wide, with a hole in the middle.

"What's this?" I ask.

"A 45 RPM of Bobby's orchestra playing *Come September.*"

"Be careful you don't break it," she warned me. "It's a collectible – might be worth a lot of money."

She never played it for us. No one we knew had a record player that would spin her oldie, but *goldie.*

Just so we wouldn't be deprived of his music, Baba scoured music stores on the coast and if none could be found, she made trips to Vancouver and ordered through the music stores. In time, we had all the CDs of Bobby Darin's great hits and played them to our heart's content for the next several years. Especially when we were in Baba's car and she blasted them with the windows wide open.

It didn't take long for me to understand why Baba never gave up listening to music from her youth.

Bobby Darin's music grew on me. But the saddest thing about him was that he had a bad heart. Yet he never stopped performing and became outspoken about wars and useless killing of people.

One evening PBS televised a special of famous singers. When Bobby Darin sang a *Simple Song of Freedom,* Baba blinked away tears and said that was probably the last concert he ever did.

Bobby Darin was only 37 when he died.

MA! DID YOU READ THE INSTRUCTIONS?

Baba never stopped dragging us along to run her errands. She always ignored my suggestions that she should do those things on her own time and not take up our playtime with her chores. She then reminded me that going out in public with her was a good way for us kids to learn to be civilized. Whatever that meant?

Once, off we went to Sears to return her vacuum cleaner that all of a sudden stopped working.

"I get no suction," she said to the young salesman. "A vacuum is useless if I can't suck up all the dirt and dust from my carpet and floors."

The salesman inserted the plug into the wall, turned the ON button on and using a small piece of carpet with bits of dirt on it, he proceeded to move the vacuum back and forth. The dirt remained on the carpet.

"See," Baba said. "I'm not making it up."

Since the unit did not do what it should, he turned it upside down to look at the rollers and as he fidgeted with this and that, he looked at Baba and with a smile said, "See here, there are two settings. One for floor rollers and one for hose with a hand-held nozzle to vacuum furniture or curtains."

"Yes, I know that," Baba said, shaking her head. "I read the pamphlet when I bought it. I know what it's suppose to do, but it's not sucking the dirt off the floor… or carpet."

With a slight grin, he pointed to the bottom of the vacuum,

"The dial was set to hose, not floor." And with that revelation, he turned the dial and proceeded to suck up all the dirt off the carpet.

"Oops," Baba said, when she realized there was nothing wrong with the unit, "I feel so stupid."

"It happens," said the sales clerk as Baba carried the vacuum to the front door.

As she strapped us into our car seats, she said, "You know, that kid in the store reminds me of your Uncle Dee."

"What does Uncle Dee have to do with your vacuum cleaner?" I asked.

"Whenever I bought the latest electronic gadget and then it would not work, I always called him – on account of I didn't have a husband to help me. But, before Dee even touched the unit he always asked, 'Ma, did you read the instructions first?'"

"Of course, I did" I always replied. "You think I'm stupid?"

"He'd look at me like I often did at him when he misbehaved and asked, '*All* of them?'"

"Obviously, you did not read all of the instructions for the vacuum, eh Baba?" I laughed.

Instead of a reply, she plunked a CD into the player and as the music started her body gyrated as if she was doing the shuffle and when a male voice rang out, she sang along…. "Yooou can have her… I..I.. don't want her… she didn't love me… anyway….."

Roy Hamilton was another great singer that Baba admired and danced to way back in the 60s. An age, and times of her life, that she continually subjected us to over the next several years.

COUPONS

Mom and Baba never agreed about the value of coupons to get a discount of ten or twenty cents off the regular price.

"Mother," Mom often said to Baba. "I don't have time to run around several stores, looking for bargains that will sit on my shelves that I won't need for months."

Baba had stacks of coupons, even those she couldn't even use with expired dates.

Whenever Baba phoned Mom, I often heard mom giving her the same response, "What's wrong, *Mother?*"

"Nothing's wrong, *daughter*. Just calling to let you know that Boursin Garlic & Chives Cheese is $4.99."

"I've already done my shopping for the week, Mother." Mom said. Whenever Mom called Baba Mother – instead of Mom or Ma – what followed was not exactly jovial.

"It's $3 off, and expiry date on the one I have is not for three months from now," Baba said.

Exasperated, Mom appeased her, "Fine, maybe I'll get some later."

"You better hurry," Baba warned her. "The sale ends tomorrow. After that, it's back to the regular price of $7.99."

"What if I buy it and I'm not in the mood for that kind of cheese?"

"How can you not be? It's the best spreadable cheese ever made," Baba said.

"Or it expires before it's eaten and I've wasted five dollars?"

"Nah. Just buy some nice whole wheat bagels and before you know it, both bagel and cheese are eaten."

"All right, Mother," she finally said. "Get me one if you're in the store."

"Okay. Maybe the kids and I'll have it for lunch tomorrow."

"Good idea, Mom. That way it won't have time to expire and end up in the compost bin."

KNIT, KNIT, KNIT

Baba's storage closet contained colourful plastic crates full of knitting yarns and a five-tier bookcase with two of the shelves stacked with slippers of various colours and sizes. Another shelf held piles of toques of solid colours, stripes and styles. She wasted no yarn and managed to coordinate quite attractive hats with many leftover bits.

"See these," she said, pointing to a bag of baby booties and hats. "These are all going to Africa."

"Are you going to Africa?" I asked.

"No, the parts where we send these knits to are not exactly a place I want to visit – too much poverty to bring back unwanted memories," she said, looking a little morose. "But, at least we can help those who don't have the opportunities we have here in Canada."

Baba's group of grannies belonged to an organization that shipped knitted layettes to parts of Africa where orphanages looked after unwanted newborn babies.

Baba learned how to knit and crochet by the time she was eight years old as a kid in Munster, Germany after *The War*, as she often referred to World War II. They were so poor – as was the rest of the world she was quick to add so as not for us to feel too sorry for her – that no piece of thread was wasted and clothes no longer wearable and mainly rags were ripped into strips and crocheted into slippers. She once showed me how they made their own crochet hooks by twiddling down a sturdy twig with a knife to smooth it out and then cut away bits at one end to form a hook.

"We then sanded the hook with a rock, removing loose bits of wood until it was nice and smooth," she said.

"Just like the cavemen did, eh Baba?" I said.

"In those days, we made do with what we had."

I know she's pretty good with a crochet hook because once she made us kids round rugs for our bedrooms. Black and red for me, and pink and purple for my sister. Mom loved them so much she asked if Baba would make her one for the hallway. Except she wanted it all white with one yellow stripe in the centre and a blue stripe half way in the circle and five feet in the round.

So off Baba took us to the thrift stores. We had three in our area so it hardly took any time before she found several good-quality white bed sheets at a reduced price. After a good soaking in hot water and bleach, they were thoroughly machine washed and dried. Once she was satisfied that no people germs remained on those sheets, she tore them into one-inch wide strips and rolled them up into large balls, all the time stripping away any loose threads. Halfway through ripping the material into strips, she had to do the rest on her balcony because the tiny particles were all over her couch and floor. And she could really see the flecks of dust flying everywhere when the sun shone through her living room window. Like snow. Not to mention she inhaled all the dust, which she didn't know about until after she was half way into the project. From then on, she wore a facemask for protection.

She spent hours and hours crocheting the rug and with every two rows of circles she'd lay it on the floor, smooth it out and then either be satisfied with it and continue to crochet one or two more rows or utter *damn* and rip out the stitches that caused it to curl.

"You said a bad word, Baba." I reminded her that swearing was not proper for us kids.

"Just watch those silly cartoons, kid," she said, "or I'll turn off the TV."

We didn't have cable at home, so I learned to ignore her cussing and focused on the screen.

"It's almost done," Baba reported her progress to Mom every few days.

In the end, it took four bed sheets – two queen size and two singles – before she told herself that it was large enough.

Finally, Baba was satisfied that the rug was finished to the best of her abilities. All single threads were pulled out and loose ends of material tucked in so they didn't stick out like a sloppy, unfinished work of art. And not one curled row bulging out of shape.

"It's me," Baba said, announcing her presence one evening as she opened our front door after ringing the bell. Up the stairs she climbed with one of those huge green garbage bags.

"Close your eyes," she ordered us. All four of us stood with our eyes closed as Baba rummaged in the bag.

"Now open," she said a few seconds later.

"Beautiful!" Mom's eyes lit up as she stared at the huge crochet rug – almost all white with a couple rounds of yellow and light blue.

Baba's round masterpiece covered the hardwood floor at the top of the stairs just outside our kitchen.

Mom loved it.

So did our cat Tiger Lily who regularly slept on it.

Baba wasn't happy that our cat spent most of her days sleeping on her white masterpiece, not caring how fast it got dirty.

"Tiger is part of our family," Mom said when Baba expressed her disdain that their pet was allowed to roam anywhere.

Several days later, Baba showed up with a small, round rug crocheted out of pink fluffy yarn. She lifted Tiger Lily, who was asleep on the white rug, laid the new small rug in the centre and plunked the cat on top of it.

"Here you go, kitty," she said to the cat. "Your own little cat rug. Now stay off the white people one!"

Once when we were at Baba's apartment watching television, she brought out a huge bag of balls of yarn. She emptied the bag on the floor and proceeded to separate them. One by one, she pulled out a ball and rolled it up, and placed it into another bag. And when she came to a snag of tangles she let out an expletive, cautiously, so we would not hear her swearing at the mess she had to fix.

"How did all that wool become so tangled up?" I lifted a clump of unrolled yarn, just a whole lot of strings intermingled.

"Have no idea, kiddo," she said. "When I put them in the bag, they were all rolled up nice and neat. Maybe a little Gremlin gets in there during the night and twists them all around just to drive me crazy. Now, it'll take me hours of untangling before I can knit you another pair of colourful socks."

During the three episodes of SpongeBob – which we loved to watch but she hated because according to her it's the loudest and most useless show on television for kids – she pulled and rolled and mumbled, "Oh, geez, what a mess... darn it... why did I ever take up knitting?"

Finally, when the balls were all rolled up, she returned the bag to her closet and said really loudly, "You guys better stay that way until I need you again!"

"Are you talking to us, Baba?" I asked. I had no idea what she meant.

"No, kid." She shook her head. "I was telling those balls of yarn to stay away from each other and not get tangled up again."

OKAY, OKAY, YOU DON'T NEED TO ASK TWICE

I once read a book called *Jacob Two Two*, written by Mordecai Richler. A very famous Canadian writer, who lived in Quebec, same province that Baba lived in way back when she was a teenager.

Mr. Richler had a son named Jacob. Jacob was part of a large family, and the only way to get any attention was to keep repeating everything twice.

Jacob Two Two became a bestseller, was made into a movie and even had a children's cartoon television series.

When Baba still lived in Ontario, she attended a function at some big theatre in Toronto when Mr. Richler was presented with a life-time achievement award for writing.

At times after that, whenever she read to us from *Jacob Two Two* or we watched a cartoon episode on television, she'd say, "I'm so glad I had a chance to meet Mr. R. before he went off to the Big Writers' Club in the sky."

I wish Mr. Richler were alive today, because my Baba had one on him.

When Baba told me to do something, once was never enough. Not even twice.

"Don't force me to move into motion," she'd warn me if I didn't obey her the first time. The second command was also ignored by us with almost as much apathy. And yet, I was kinda on the verge of preparing myself to move. But when the same words came out of Baba's mouth for the third time, she really meant business and consequences were about to be bestowed upon me.

So, I had only two choices: one – obey Baba's command from the get-go, or two, bring on the waterworks – mine.

Most of the time I grudgingly obeyed. Sometimes I threatened Baba with, "I'm telling Mom and Dad that you yelled at me," and would burst into tears. Sometimes fake ones.

So, Mr. Mordecai, in your life, your son was ignored to point of repetition.

In mine, we ignored our Baba as much as we could get away with.

REMEMBRANCE DAY
IS EVERY DAY

At the first sight of the Royal Canadian Legion Veterans standing outside of shopping malls with boxes of poppies, Baba's demeanour towards life changes.

Her eyes start to water and to cover up that she might burst into tears, she blinks her eyes rapidly and sniffs the tears away.

She's in awe, especially of the old guys in war uniforms. They stand tall, proudly displaying many medals pinned to their lapels and chests. Their hands, aged with wrinkles and some gnarled with arthritis, clutching boxes of red poppies.

"Would you like a cup of hot coffee?" Baba asked an elderly man smiling at us.

"No, thank you," he replied. "I just had my lunch break, so I'm fine."

Baba dropped a coin into the slot of the box, lifted a poppy out of it and still blinking, she said, "Thank you."

She then turned away and offered me a coin. I also dropped it into the slot and took a poppy.

Baba told me that she gets very emotional when Remembrance Day comes around each year; it's as if she's in another life and stays there until November 12th.

"Tomorrow is Remembrance Day," she announced. "We're going to the Canadian Legion for laying of the wreaths ceremony. Hope it doesn't rain."

On the morning of November 11th, we dressed for outdoors.

"We need to get there early to stand right next to the cenotaph so we can see what's going on," she said. "And, it's very important that you kids behave yourself and respect what the day stands for."

My not quite five-year-old brain didn't grasp her meaning. But over the years she drilled into our heads the reason why this day was so important: freedom.

As we dressed in double layers of winter snowsuits and snow boots, Athena wouldn't stop fidgeting.

Baba was getting agitated. She pulled Athena's boot on and zipped it up. Just as the second boot was about to be zipped, Athena kicked the first one off. And then giggled. Oh, goody, I'm driving Baba crazy. And then Baba sniffed the air once, twice and uttered, "Oh, crap." My fifteen-month old sister needed a diaper change.

Baba's face scrunched up as she was about to give Athena a lecture on using the bathroom before putting on a snowsuit, then realized that her granddaughter had not yet developed control of her bodily functions or had the ability to predict urges. Instead, Baba heaved a sigh, removed her own winter boots and dropped her jacket to the floor.

She hoisted Athena onto her hip and off they went to the bedroom. When they returned Baba fitted a pink and purple Russian-style winter hat onto Athena's head. As Baba tucked Athena's arms into the jacket, the Velcro ripped and the hat dropped to the floor.

"Oh, oh," Athena said with a grin. The kid was having fun and Baba looked like she was about to cry.

Finally, we're both strapped into our car seats of Baba's purple Hyundai Accent.

"Everyone ready?" Baba said and inhaled deeply as if she was preparing for a race of a lifetime. Three minutes later, we parked along a side road, and Baba dug out the stroller from the trunk. In went Athena and off we went.

It was a frosty and sunny morning. The parking lot at the Royal Canadian Legion was jammed with cars and people. Baba's plan for a good standing spot in front was not to be, on account of the ceremony being half over. On account of you-know-who pooped her pants and made us late.

But I managed to squeeze in by the bushes, with a good view of the uniformed Cadets standing at attention and the local high school band. (Roughly ten years later, I played horn in that band and by then I knew all about what Remembrance Day stood for.)

Men and women in war uniforms stood erect, as they lined the path to the cenotaph.

A few feet away from us, was a very old man – who looked almost like he should be dead – in a wheelchair, with a blanket covering his lap. He was dressed in full army uniform. The front of his jacket was decorated with a whole slew of medals, most likely awarded him for his bravery in fighting the enemy.

A man next to me whispered to his young son, *He's from the First World War.*

"Look, Baba," I said as the assistant removed the blanket and helped the old man slowly rise to his feet. "He's alive."

Baba shushed me to be quiet and murmured, "Have some respect for your elders."

Perhaps they wheeled the old man to parade him in front of us young people to remind us what sacrifices were made in the war. So that we have the freedom to "play with those silly video games and watch garbage on television", as Baba reminded me so many times, over the years.

My eyes were fixed on the wheelchair as ever so slowly, the old soldier stood erect – as erect as a body can stand when it's crippled with age and arthritis. He raised his hand to the top of his head and offered a salute. And as the bugler ended his last note, the hand slowly lowered and again the War Hero sat in the wheelchair to rest his frail body.

Perhaps he's thinking of decades earlier, as he and so many other young men hid in the muddy trenches, rifles ready to take down the approaching enemy. Maybe now he wonders whether he would live long enough to repeat this, next year.

A voice over the microphone announced names of wreath donors. For the next while, family members made their way towards the cenotaph to lay a green wreath, decorated with red poppies, for their loved ones – who gave their lives, so we could live.

My baby sister, thumb in mouth, slept through it all. She was nice and cozy, covered with a pink and purple car blanket that Baba crocheted.

During the whole ceremony, Baba sniffed a few times. Once she took a wad of neatly folded clean tissues out of her jacket pocket and removed two tissues. With one tissue she wiped away her tears, blew her nose and deposited the used tissue into the clean unused one, and folded the germs away into a plastic baggy. Then out of another plastic bag she took out a small bottle of hand sanitizer, squirted a couple of drops onto the palm of her hand and rubbed away all the germs that might have gotten stuck to her hands. Which she says, is how germs are passed on to others when people don't wash their hands to rid germy bacteria.

Baba's little bottle came out often when we were outdoors, especially after an outing in the playground with me swinging on the monkey bars. And most definitely before I got into the car and distributed all those other peoples' germs.

After the ceremony, everyone's invited to a presentation inside the Legion Hall, followed by a lunch of sandwiches made by the Women's Auxiliary.

"We'll go inside next year," Baba said, when we got into the car and headed out to Tim Horton's for lunch, "when Athena is walking and I don't have to cart her stroller around."

"You know, Alex," Baba said, while we enjoyed a bowl of chicken soup and my favourite doughnut oozing with cherry jelly. "If those brave men and women did not fight the enemy, we would not be here. Many of the young soldiers gave their lives in battle, so we can enjoy a life of freedom."

"Where would we be, Baba?" I asked. Her talk of freedom often confused me. I never felt that my freedom was in any way threatened.

"Well…," she started, and then said, "you know, maybe I'll wait a couple years before I boggle your young mind with descriptive scenes of war and carnage."

"And just so you know, kid," she reminded me, "for me, every day in Canada is Remembrance Day."

With time, I started to understand her retelling of life during World War II.

I thought Baba was born in Canada. She didn't speak with any type of a European accent. When she moved here out west, I just assumed she was born there – in Ontario. But, Baba was born in Ukraine. In June 1944, her parents – my great-grandparents – four older sisters, a brother and a six-month old baby, fled their home as Stalin's Russian armies raided villages. Those who refused to join Stalin and his Communist regime, were shot to death, their homes burned down to ash.

In the middle of the night, Baba and her family crossed the Ukrainian border into Romania, and for weeks they trekked through the Carpathian Mountains, always aware that if found, Stalin would herd them back home to toil on work farms or be shipped off to Siberia.

With the help of other freedom fighters, Baba's family survived and ended up in a Displaced Persons Camp in Munster, Germany. For almost five years they lived in fear of being deported back to Ukraine. But fortune smiled upon them, and on February 23, 1949, Baba and her family immigrated to Canada. Baba was nine years old.

Later, she showed me their province of Chernovtsi in Ukraine on the world map. With her finger, she drew an imaginary trek through Romania, Austria and Germany, and across the Atlantic Ocean. And finally, with a deep sigh she pointed to Halifax, Nova Scotia.

"In *Kanada*," she said. "Pier 21. Land of the free."

And don't you ever forget it, she reminded me often enough.

As I got older, I got it. I think. I could somewhat understand why it means so much for her to commemorate Remembrance Day, November 11th, of each year.

When I asked if she ever felt sad about the hardships her family went through during World War II, she replied that almost every person in Europe went through some sort of hell. But, here she was, her family intact and alive and doing fine.

"You know, if my family perished in Ukraine and didn't come

to Canada," she said, "you and I wouldn't be here talking about all this."

"What do you mean I wouldn't be here?" I said. "Where would I be?"

"There would be no you," she said with a chuckle and then added, "I'm just kidding you, kiddo. But I am very fortunate to be here to drive my grandkids crazy."

She must have realized that she shouldn't have said that and as I got older she managed to un-boggle my mind with plausible explanations of life.

I don't think I'll ever really understand how our great-grand-parents suffered, so that future generations – mine – enjoyed a life of freedom.

BABA'S TALE
– UKRAINE –
1944

NICHOLAS AND TARAS

Papa was a devoted husband and father. And a devout Christian and a loyal neighbour.

We were a mid-size family with five daughters and a son. Papa should have had three sons to help work the farm, but it wasn't to be.

Mama almost died giving birth to twin boys. The one that came out first only lived for a day. The other never uttered a sound, even after the midwife smacked it on its bottom a couple of times, just in case he was holding back. It didn't help, though. Not one peep. Poor little thing never even had a chance to take a single breath. And just as Papa and Mama were preparing for its burial, the other twin decided to join his brother.

A carpenter by trade, Papa built a fine coffin of the best pine available.

"Make sure you get enough wood to make it large enough for both of them," Mama said, as Papa hitched the wagon for the lumberyard.

Mama said they came into the world together, they must also go out together. Since they would never be with the rest of the family on earth, they should at least keep each other company in heaven.

Mama lined the coffin with a feather quilt. Soft cream-colored cotton, stuffed with fine goose feathers.

"To keep our sons warm in the winter." Mama had a hard time

holding back tears as she dressed her dead babies in white cotton gowns, and tied lace bonnets around their heads.

My dead brothers were baptized Nicholas and Taras.

Well, not baptized really, because the Orthodox Church did not baptize dead babies, but Mama didn't care. She gave them each their names and did her own baptism with the sign of the cross over them, ending with an Amen. And a whole lot of tears.

Nicholas was named for our Saint Nicholas who was kind to children and brought them gifts during the Orthodox Christmas week.

Taras was named after Taras Shevchenko, the most famous of all Ukrainian poets.

Mama covered Nicholas and Taras with a hand-embroidered tablecloth and tucked the ends underneath the featherbed.

"The Lord gives and the Lord takes away," said the Minister at the graveside. He too defied the church and blessed the coffin with holy water.

It was a damp morning with rain coming down in a light drizzle. Papa and Mama held onto each other for comfort. As the box was lowered into the ground, wild noises came out of Mama's throat. She took a step towards the pit. Was she going to jump in after her two babies? But Papa held her back.

"Olena, please. Please don't. There's nothing you can do. It is God's will. They will be safe in His hands, up there in Heaven."

Up there on the hill, two wooden crosses mark the single grave.

The mourners turned away from the graveside and made their way slowly down the hill towards our house. Papa and Mama still huddled close to each other. Mama long ago stopped her wailing, just soft whimpering sounds could be heard as her chest heaved with each breath she took. The pain of loss was slowly dulling as fatigue took over.

That night at dinner Papa said his usual prayer. He thanked God for the sun, the healthy farm animals, those tasty chicken eggs and for that fine rooster who has been doing such a good job keeping the chickens happy. Oh, yes, and thank you for relieving the pain from my back, finally. For our bountiful harvests of the past and those yet to come, for the rain – but not all in one day, spread it around where and when it's needed. And please God, keep a close watch on our two sons. Olena and I lay them in your hands now, our two angels. Bless them God, forever and ever, Amen.

After dinner Papa went outside, leaving Mama alone to tend to her grief in her own way.

Mr. Petrenko walked along the path towards Papa. They shook hands and hugged each other. The Petrenkos knew the feeling of loss too well. Saveta Petrenko almost died giving birth a year earlier. A son, stillborn, is also buried up on the hill overlooking their cornfield.

Papa and Mr. Petrenko sat on tree stumps near a woodpile at the side of the house. An earthen jug of homemade corn vodka passed between the two neighbours. Each took a swig and handed it back to the other.

The sun slowly disappeared beyond the horizon.

"You thinking we may have a hot summer this year?" Mr. Petrenko said.

"Would be nice for a change."

"Yes, that it would be."

"The wheat fields need plenty of sun."

"And plenty of rain. For what good are acres of parched land to a farmer, I ask you, oy?"

"But we don't need a whole month's worth of rain all in one day."

"Tak ,(yes) tak. There's no need to drown the crops."

"And have our family perish from hunger over the winter."

"And what about hay for the animals?"

"Yep."

"Yep, sure need many bales of hay stashed in the barn to tide us over the cold winter months."

Both men shook their heads in disagreement, nodded in agreement, and passed the jug for another swig of vodka.

"I will need to borrow your plough tomorrow or maybe the next day, if you're not using it," Mr. Petrenko said.

"What's wrong with yours? Did your wife wear it out last year?" Papa laughed. It was the first time Papa laughed since his twin sons died.

"You must be joking, my friend. When she married me, she said, 'You want a horse to pull the plough, then you get yourself a horse. It's enough that I'm willing to give you children, clean your house and cook your meals, you should be thankful for that,' she warned me. No, Saveta didn't wear out my plough. She never even touched it once. It's an old plough, the handle rusted from overuse and snapped in two. The blacksmith in town, well, he's taking his time fixing it. I should have looked after it over the winter months, but I didn't, so now I have to wait. It should be ready in a few days. In the meantime, if you're not using yours, for a few hours..."

"Sure, of course, you may borrow the plough. Any time, help yourself."

The last few drops of the vodka were shared. The jug was dry. Time to get some sleep, for daylight comes early and the fields don't seed themselves.

"Good night, my friend," Papa said.

"And a good night to you too, my patrone."

The men embraced, patting each other lightly on the back. A comforting gesture. A quiet evening, with only crickets heard here and there. Papa stumbled a little as he walked towards the house. His shadow is reflected in the moonlight. Papa looked up into the clear sky and noticed two bright stars twinkling silently.

"Good-bye, my sons," Papa sniffed away the urge to cry again.

"Shush," Papa reminded the creaking front door not to disturb his sleeping family.

Mama was snoring gently, curled up on her side of the double bed. All those tears sure must have tired her out. Not to mention giving birth to two sons and then see them both die just like that. At thirty-eight, Mama's strong constitution pulled her through at birthing time. But not her two sons. No way of knowing how God worked. And why He takes little children before they even have a chance to learn how to crawl?

Papa removed his overalls and knelt by the bedside. He crossed himself once and mumbled a prayer. Quiet like, to himself, so as not to wake anyone.

"I hope you hear me God. I know, I know, you must be tired of all my praying. But if I can't pray to you, then what's the point of my bothering to waste my time talking to the wind."

Papa crossed himself for the second time.

"If there was someone else I could pray to I would, but there isn't, so you get elected every time. Maybe you should appoint an assistant to help you out. Although I can't imagine anyone praying to an assistant God. For there is only one You.

"You may be surprised, God, but tonight I'm not asking any more favours. Enough is enough, I say. I'm too tired and so drained out. Maybe you're punishing me for bothering you too much. Is that why you took my two sons? I don't know how you work. One day you give and the next day you take away. Such a mystery. Anyway, God, I know you will take care of our two precious babies. So, I'm not saying another word. Just goodnight God, and have a good sleep."

Papa made the sign of the cross for the third time and then lay next to Mama and promptly fell into a deep sleep.

MOM! HELP ME!

My sister Athena and I sat at the dining table set with a large platter stacked with crepes, jars of strawberry jam, chocolate syrup, organic maple syrup and a compote Baba made that morning from frozen blueberries – with "a good squirt of lemon juice to enhance the flavour." We were in for a breakfast feast.

It was Saturday morning and Baba was making us breakfast on account of Mom and Dad were away in Vancouver for a business event the night before and stayed overnight in a hotel. Baba always slept over with us when our parents were away overnight and that meant we were subjected to almost two full days of her lectures. No breaks.

But she did make great pancakes for breakfast, and lunch was always out at a restaurant of our choosing. The one time we were allowed to eat what Mom called "useless fast food with zero nutritional value."

Baba said if our parents can party away without us, we should also treat ourselves when they're not here and since we don't know what they ate or drank, it is none of their business what we eat or drink. Lucky for Baba, Mom's theory of "don't ask, can't do anything about it now anyway" always saved her, and us, from possible lying.

Most of the time, these outings of eating forbidden foods were prefaced with warnings of, "Sure, you can have a double-bubble wad of sugary gum, but don't tell your parents. You don't need to lie, you know – just don't offer any more information than you can get away with. Sometimes, even *I don't remember* would work. And, that's really not a lie. But, if you always tell the truth, you never have to remember what you said or did not say."

Quite often when Baba went on and on with her tirades about whatever, I tried to ignore her by walking away, but this day we were stuck with her until my parents came home.

"You know," she said, taking a sip of coffee, "if you ever fall down and hurt yourself, who's the one person you yell for help?"

"Okay, Baba, who's the person we yell for?" I said, smothering a pancake with chocolate sauce.

"Your Mother," she said. "We always yell for our mothers when we are in trouble."

Trouble? What trouble? I had no idea what she was talking about, but as I took a drink of orange juice I gave it some thought.

"Oh yeah," I said. "Now I get it. Once when I lost control on my skis and flew off course I remember yelling "Mom! Stop Me!"

"Exactly. We never yell for our Dad, it's always our Mother. I guess it's because she gave birth to us and we have that personal connection."

Oh, oh, here comes another long-winded narrative.

"I have to tell you a funny story," she said. "Well, it's not really funny, but... Anyway, a couple weeks ago, I was in the shower and as I reached over for the scrubby my foot missed the plastic mat with suction cups and I slipped on the wet porcelain and went flying. In a split second, I had no control of where or how I was going to fall. But I knew I was definitely falling, so instinctively I grabbed the shower curtain and as I felt myself lowering my body, the rod holding the shower curtain released itself from the walls and next thing I'm aware of is my legs are in the tub, and I'm leaning backwards on the edge – and the top part of my body is on the floor outside the tub all tangled up in the plastic curtain."

"I don't think there's anything funny about you falling in the tub," I said.

She took another sip of coffee and went on.

"As I lay there, not moving, I realized what happened and all I could think of was: did I break my back? And if I did break any bones, how was I ever going to crawl out of the tub and get to my phone in the living room and maybe call the ambulance. And then, ever so slowly, I started to move parts of arms and legs and realized nothing was broken. With a sigh of relief and a huge 'Thank You, God!' I crossed myself and managed to crawl out of the tub."

"Did you call out for your Mother?" I said.

"I don't remember and even if I had, it would have done no good. My mother has been dead for decades. Although, you know if we believe that our deceased parents are always looking out for us, maybe my mother was there with me when I fell and that's probably why I never broke any bones."

"Like a Guardian Angel, eh, Baba?" Athena said.

"Yeah, kiddo. And I really believe that we all have one."

Then she said, "Weeks later, after several medical treatments for bruises on my back – which I didn't break – I told your mother. You know what she said?"

"What did Mom say?" I asked.

"She said, "Oh Mother, why didn't you call me?'"

"And what would you have done if I did call," Baba asked Mom.

"Nothing, I guess," Mom replied after giving it some thought.

"And, that's why I didn't call her," Baba said to us, as she shoved a forkful of crepe into her mouth.

A MATCHING PAIR

Almost half a century ago, when Baba and grandpa were just married, they lived in a high-rise apartment building in Scarborough, Ontario.

"One day," Baba said, "I entered the elevator on the eleventh floor and was greeted by a doctor on his way down to the lobby.

"Dr. Green was a surgeon at Scarborough General Hospital. Tall, with baby blue eyes and blond hair he turned many a head," so Baba said. "But he was married with a baby on the way, so my girlfriends and I admired him from afar.

"After exchanging "good mornings" I looked down to the floor and noticed that the doctor wore identical styled shoes on both feet. Penny loafers. But the left loafer was black and the right one was navy.

"I wasn't really rude, you know," she said. "Maybe a little nosey and I was known to at times criticize how people dressed. But I would never insult the men and women in the medical field."

Really, Baba? I wanted to say, you do not criticize? Ha!

"Okay, maybe I'm a little critical when I don't agree with something. But this was different. I didn't want to hurt his feelings, but I felt it was my duty to point out the difference to the sharply-dressed doctor. What if he had to perform some sort of organ transplant on a patient that day? I had to test him and hope to high heavens that he knew his right from his left, before he removed a healthy kidney. And possibly got sued for malpractice.

"So I coughed a couple of times as if clearing my throat and said, 'Excuse me, Dr. Green, I don't mean to point out the flaws in your dress, but do you know that you have one black and one navy shoe on'?"

"'Pardon?" said the doctor, furrowing his brow. He was very sharply-dressed in a stylish French cut, navy blue suit, with a Toronto Maple Leafs tie knotted around the collar of a crisp, purple-coloured shirt.

"Your shoes." I pointed to the floor. "They're not the same."

"'Really?' said the surprised doctor. And when he looked down to his feet and noticed the difference, he simply shrugged his shoulders.

"And then, grinning sheepishly at me he added, 'When I get home tonight, I must check my closet. I might have *another* pair just like them, somewhere back there.'

"By the time I realized the humour of it all," Baba said, "the handsome doctor was off the elevator and I was left to my own chuckling."

One morning as I dressed for school, I rummaged through my messy sock drawer searching for a rolled-up ball of a matching pair, but found none, except for several odd mismatched socks. So, I grabbed two different types of knee socks that Baba had knit. One with yellow and green stripes and the other sock, green with yellow stripes. Sounds like they should be the same, but they weren't, both of different shades of green and yellow. Anyway I thought they looked cool.

So, as I'm walking towards my second-grade classroom an older kid looked at my legs and when he realized the different patterns and colours of my socks he asked: "Hey, Kid! Do you know that your socks don't match?"

I could not resist. "Yes, I do," I said with a wide grin. "And I have another pair just like them at home in my sock drawer."

The kid opened his mouth and then realized how ridiculous it would have been for him to say anything and that maybe he asked a stupid question. Instead, he just shook his head and walked away.

I'm definitely going to wear the other mismatched pair another day and see if he notices the difference.

HOW DO YOU SPELL DICTIONARY?

"In the 1970s when your Mom was around three," Baba said, "your grandfather answered the doorbell and there stood a door-to-door salesman with a huge briefcase, bulging with his wares."

"In those days, door-to-door salesmen were very common. An hour or so later, when the salesman left, your Granddad had in his possession a purchase order for a complete set of 24 volumes of Encyclopaedia, so that your mother and her brother would have ready-reference guides at their fingertips, right there in our home. And no need to trek all the way to the Public Library – especially in the winter with all that snow in Ontario – when working on a school project that required new information not stored in their brains.

"Back then, having a set of beautifully-bound, leather-like reference books was a sign of intelligence," Baba said. "Even though after flipping through the pages once or twice they just gathered dust on make-shift bookcases of wooden planks set on adjustable stacks of bricks that lined a complete wall of the family room in our basement.

"And now, thrift stores are loaded with those must-have books that you kids think are outdated.

"A few days later, a huge box was delivered by Canada Post and thus began your mother's dive into her knowledge of the unknown," Baba said.

"For the next 10 years or so, once a year we also received a heavy issue summarizing the most important or weird goings-on of world events for the year gone by.

"As a member of this exclusive club of book buyers, Granddad also bought a series of how-to instruction books. How to paint your house without hiring a painter. How to grow vegetables even though you may live in a high-rise apartment building. How to sew your own clothes. How to fix a leaky faucet without the expense of a plumber – although not always advisable as some men found out when more damage was done to their home. How to become a regular Mister Fix-it after following all the instructions contained in these books. Self-education. No need to spend time and money going to proper educational institutions to earn a degree in fixer-uppers."

Baba told me that the best investment was how an amateur could learn to electrically wire your house properly without being educated in an electricians' college and earning a proper Electrical Certificate. "However," she added with a grin, "there was no guarantee that you wouldn't burn the house down for lack of experience in electronics."

* * * * *

Uncle Dee loved those instruction books, and when he grew older he taught himself about simple maintenance – like smoothing over a wall after Baba tore down the wallpaper she no longer wanted and left holes that needed to be plugged up before re-painting. Years later, when my grandparents were selling their house, Dee learned how to rip up all the unwanted wall-to-wall carpeting and with a rented sander he refinished the hardwood floors to a perfect shine. And made the new buyers very happy that they bought a spotless house.

* * * * *

As a special gift for being the first – so the salesman said – in their neighbourhood to purchase these sought-after encyclopaedias, they received a freebie. A huge, four inches thick, 9x12, hardcover dictionary titled, *Unabridged Edition of The Random House Dictionary of the English Language.*

Printed in the United States of America in 1967, the tome contained 2,059 pages of information: French, German, Spanish dictionary of everyday terms, governments, famous parks, rivers, mileages to and from major cities, and even waterfalls of the world. It also had style of writing and usage of punctuation.

I particularly enjoyed the Atlas section. Sixty-four pages of colourful maps of countries on each continent around the world with a Gazetteer for quick reference. Each page had its own listings of dominant land use in agriculture, industries and resources as they were back then, until 1965 or so.

Page 44, C5, listed Chernovtsi – Baba's place of birth – in Russia, when Ukraine was still ruled by the U.S.S.R.

And listings of major events in chronological order from *c3200 – 2780 bc* from *Rise of the first dynasties in Egypt* to *December 9, 1965, Pope Paul VI formally closes Ecumenical Council Vatican II.*

I know I could have educated myself about past historical events just by reading the dictionary and not ever going to school. Maybe. Or, maybe not.

That dictionary was Baba's saviour for decades and even though she had moved roughly ten times since she acquired it, it always came with her. It cost a mint to ship, she often complained.

I was fascinated with a single page, glued into the inside front cover of the dictionary. Its title, Indo-European Languages, listed every variation of world languages and their origin. For example, Ukrainian language was part of Slavonic and further broken down into East Slavic.

Ukrainian is Baba's first language. Every letter written is pronounced with its own meaning – never changing. It is, what it is, Baba said.

"The English language always puzzled and often frustrated me," Baba said. "In Canada, learning a new language when I was nine years old I had to know how to spell a word before I could write it correctly. Or even to look it up in the dictionary for the correct spelling. One example is the word enough – why not spell it enuf? Go figger, eh?"

I totally agreed with Baba. I also wasted a lot time looking for the correct meaning of a word that sounded nothing like its spelling – phonetically.

"Another mind-boggler was the simple word **tee** – the gadget where a golfer places a ball before hopefully smacking it into a hole," Baba said. "The other word, sounding exactly the same is **tea** – a drink enjoyed with jam and bread. The second **e** is replaced by an **a**. Why?"

In Baba's language, tea is **chai**, a unique word which is and always will be the stuff people drink after steeping some dead leaves in a pot of hot boiling water.

When I tried to write some Russian letters of the alphabet, Baba chastised me, "Why do you want to learn that Communist language?" It was as if I were going against her upbringing and disrespecting my heritage.

So, I switched to the Greek – on account of we often go to Daphne's Greek Restaurant for dinner and I practised writing that alphabet off the menu.

And Arabic – just because the letters were so strange.

Anyway, I doubt either one of those countries harmed Baba's people during The War.

But a few days later, she handed me a very thin 3-ring binder. Inside were some blank pages of ruled paper for writing and photocopies of the Greek and Arabic alphabets. And a sheet of Cyrillic – both Ukrainian and Russian – alphabets. Each foreign letter had its English equivalent written beside it.

"I thought you didn't want me to write Russian?" I asked Baba.

"The letters are somewhat the same as Ukrainian," she said. "Maybe one day you'll travel abroad, it can't hurt to know more than what you know."

I'd sit for hours, copying the foreign alphabets into my own created words, most I would normally not be exposed to.

That exposure to the alphabets of *foreign* languages became quite valuable in high school, and I did select Russian in grade eleven.

The dictionary sat on a table in Baba's bedroom, not far from her desk and laptop. It is always opened to the last page of information she checked out.

There are dried flowers between some pages, notes scribbled on pieces of papers, and a photo or two of days gone by. Several articles she had written for local magazines in Ontario. But mostly *Letters to the Editor* that were published in local newspapers. She sure accumulated a lot of tidbits in the past forty years.

Baba claimed she has no use for the Internet. She gets all the information she needs right there at her fingertips. Unless, of course, she needs to know current usages of words that were invented after the computer age came into being, which was not that long ago. Then she reluctantly turns on her laptop, calls up the Internet and surfs the Web.

I once asked Baba if I could take the huge Dictionary home.

"I schlepped that tome with me all over the country all these years, so it's staying put," she said. Then added, "I'll leave it to you in my will."

"Why do you often say *schlep* – it's a Jewish word. I though you were enemies in the war."

"The Jewish race was not our enemy. Bad guys were our enemies. Anyway, *schlep* has become a universal term. It sounds good, needs no explanation. I'm sure the Jewish people forgive us for borrowing it."

"Gees, Baba," I said. "If you live as long as you claim you will, by then I won't need it."

"Yes, you will, kid," she said. "This dictionary will never go out of style. And if your kids ever wonder what it was like back in the olden days, when their great-grandparents were around, it's right there at your fingertips."

At the speed of information these days, I wonder if we'll ever flip through pages of paper books again. I sure hope so.

Hopefully even in the far future, everything old will be new again.

BABA'S TALE
– UKRAINE –
1944

MY CHORES

From the time I learned to walk, I was assigned chores. It was my daily duty to search out the chicken coop for eggs. Each morning at sunrise, I would run into the barn and while the chickens cackled and flew around, I gathered fresh eggs into a basket. Sometimes I came back into the house with poop-covered straw in my hair that Mama proceeded to wash out in a porcelain basin of water.

Papa needed a hearty breakfast each morning. Eggs, slabs of fried bacon and slices of freshly baked bread with churned butter and jam. A hot steamy cup of tea and Papa was set for the morning's toil.

At the first sign of spring and the last of the snow melted, Papa tilled the land.

Our modest farm of several acres had rows of corn and wheat. Also patches of cabbage, beets, potatoes, beans and peas, onions, tomatoes and turnips. We had no need to shop in town for vegetables. We grew any plant that thrived in our soil. Even unwanted weeds.

GOOSE FEATHERS

Mama should have been a butcher. Especially when it came to chickens, ducks or geese. When a goose was good and plump, Mama laid it on the wooden chopping block and with a quick swish overhead, the hatchet came down. Just one good whack was enough to separate the fowl's head from the tip of the neck. Blood squirted all over the place: on the ground, in the air, even onto Mama. Sometimes the chicken got away and ran around in circles with its head cut off. But it never went too far and would soon be caught, giving up its life for us to enjoy in a meal. Next, Mama held its neck over a bucket to drain the blood out of it. When the chicken no longer had any life in it, Mama sat on a stool, secured its legs between her thighs and proceeded to pluck all the feathers out of its skin.

The feathers were washed in warm soapy water in a basin and laid out on a clean bed sheet in the sun to dry. Once the feathers were dry, the fine plumage was ripped off the long stems and stored in a cotton sack. After we've had our fill of eating chickens, geese or ducks, we had an ample supply of soft feathers to stuff a pillow or a feather quilt that kept us warm in the winter.

When we ate more chickens and geese than we had use for the feathers, Mama brought them into town and sold them to the well-to-do ladies who enjoyed sleeping on soft beds, but wouldn't dare touch a fowl unless it was fully roasted. Mama made a nice profit from the sale of her feathers. When a new dress or a pair of shavary (pants for men) were needed, Mama used her feather money to purchase material at the fabric shop.

PRAY FOR RAIN

Sometimes Papa had a special request. After too many sunny days, Papa asked God for a good heavy rain so we wouldn't have to lug pails of water from the nearby creek to keep the crops from drying out.

At other times, Papa told God to hold back the rain and bring out the sun.

"Dear God," Papa watched the downpour from the sky as it flooded the cornfield. "It's been raining four days and four nights. Enough with the waterworks, already. Please God, you're going to drown us out."

"Maybe God wants us to build an Ark," Mama said.

"Who knows what God wants us to do? But if this rain doesn't stop, our crops will be ruined."

Sometimes God answered Papa's prayers. But at other times God must have been too busy listening to other peoples' prayers.

I prayed that the next time Papa went to town, he'd bring me some sweets. Or pencils and paper to draw with. Or a new doll.

Once, I prayed that Mama would not take my pet pig to the slaughter house. But I loved smoked bacon and Mama convinced me that pigs weren't meant to be house pets. Unless I wanted to clean up after them, which I didn't.

Or, I prayed that God would come and take my older sister away. Especially when she wouldn't let me play with her friends and locked me in the barn. But He never heard me, for she was always around.

And sometimes I even asked God to make it rain for another day, so I didn't have to do some of my chores.

When it rained, Papa and Mama couldn't work in the fields so they tended to feeding the animals. And I got to stay indoors and sleep all I wanted, so much that I soon got tired from sleeping too long.

It seems at times that when God answered my prayer, He ignored Papa's request. I guess we confused God with all the different things we asked for in our prayers.

OFF TO THE MARKET

Saturdays were spent in town at the market, where Mama would peddle her freshly churned butter, cheese and cream. Or sell farm animals that *we had more than enough to see us over the winter months.*

We'd rise at first crack of dawn and help Papa load a two-wheel pushcart and whoever felt like spending a day away from the farm would join in and trek a kilometre into town.

At the market, we'd set up our stall and Mama settled in for the sale. Mama enjoyed catching up on the latest gossip with the other women who brought their products to sell and get away from farm chores.

While Mama peddled her wares, Papa ran errands. Shoes were taken to the cobbler to be resoled. Papa loved roaming through the lumberyard. Should he make a new chair for Mama's kitchen? Or replace a worn-out plank of wood in the pushcart?

At harvest time, sunflower seeds and bags of fresh-picked corn were taken to the town mill. The miller dumped a bag of sunflower seeds into a grinder and produced a jug of freshly-squeezed oil for cooking.

The corn kernels were stripped off the thick ear stems and ground into cornmeal. A grain, much coarser than flour for bread, was our daily staple. Mamalega, a cornmeal hash cooked in a pot of boiling water, was stirred constantly to prevent burning on the bottom of the pot. When the mixture became too thick to stir any further, the pot was turned over onto a platter. We ate mamalega every day, as a substitute for potatoes, rice or noodles. My favourite dessert was hot mamalega topped with a mixture of sour cream and plum jam.

In town, all chores done, Papa joined the other husbands. Many of them just relaxing in the shade, waiting for their wives to finish their marketing.

Whatever produce Mama did not sell that day, was brought back home and slopped into the trough to fatten up our pig, who needed all her strength after giving birth to baby piglets.

But planting vegetables in the spring of 1944 was a waste of our time. For no sooner than the green shoots sprouted through the earth, they were abandoned.

There was no corn to harvest, or wheat to gather, or sweet peas to shell. Our farm that for decades was tended by Mama's loving hands and Papa's sweat, was left behind as we fled our home to save our lives.

And Papa had more reasons to hate Stalin.

BE CAREFUL WHAT
YOU WISH FOR

Watch what you wish for, they say. Who *they* are, is one big mystery. The other mystery being why we have no choice in choosing our relatives. And, in many cases, without even a proper invitation to feel free to stick their nose into our daily life, they do.

So as not to insult the visitor who, after all, will go home soon, we allow them to disrupt our status quo, if only just for a day or two.

A good example of such visiting relatives are our grandparents.

Yes, I was fortunate to have known – and still do – all my four grandparents.

My dad's father lived thousands of miles away in Ontario, with yearly visits.

My Nana lived on Vancouver Island and ferried into our lives once a month, or so.

My Mom's father also lived in Ontario and would visit once every two years, or when he missed his daughter and grandkid, namely me, and later on my kid sister.

All three grandparents had one thing in common. They came for a vacation, we partied, they dined us at local restaurants and bought us tons of treats. And, when they had enough of us – and we, not so much enough of them – they went home. Until months or years later, they'd show up again with opened arms and great welcomes.

But, in my case there's that other kind of relative. My dad's dreaded mother-in-law. My mother's mother. Our Baba.

Baba also lived in Ontario and visited us yearly. But when I was three, she swooped in on us. Like, literally. And thought herself as some sort of a Mary Poppins – add on almost 40 years, plus 40 pounds.

But unlike the famous Disney Nanny who left after just a short visit after reminding the family members to love each other, Baba stayed and stayed. And stayed. For what seemed like, at the time, eons.

For the next ten years we were in for a roller coaster ride – with Baba in the driver's seat who sometimes went out of control and nothing could stop her.

Sometimes I could really have done without Baba hanging around, ordering us to do this, don't do that, wash our hands.

Don't you dare wipe your nose on your sleeve. Use a tissue! And then wash your hands! Again! With soap!

One day, after being with us for about two years I could no longer stand Baba's nagging and out of the blue, I yelled back at her, "I wish you were dead!"

As the words came out of my mouth, I wished with all my might that I had not said them. But I did. Out of anger and frustration. I wished my Baba dead.

In a flash, this terrible thought went through my mind.

What if I could really wish someone to die? And I couldn't take the wish back.

Then I wished for Aladdin and his magic lamp to miraculously appear before me and please, please, grant me just one wish. At the time, I had no use for the other two wishes. But I would definitely wish that Baba did not die. Just maybe move away, thousands of miles away, and just come for regular yearly visits. Like the other grandparents who knew their place in our lives. And, don't forget the treats.

But alas, Aladdin did not appear and I was stuck with the thought that my Baba would die. And I would burn in Hell for eternity, on account of my wish came true. As horrible as it was, I wished my old Baba dead and there she would lie in a casket, ready to be lowered six feet into the ground forever to rot, with tiny bugs making their way into the pine wood and nibbling at her flesh.

It would be no surprise to me, if at least one of those pesky gnats spat out bits of Baba's flesh. "This is one bad-tasting Momma, dude. I bet everyone did the happy dance at this old lady's funeral."

When those earth bugs had enough, all that would be left of my Baba were naked, meatless, dried-up bones. Just like the dinosaur fossils palaeontologists dig up in the ruins of Egypt, on the Discovery Channel on television.

So when Mom came home, Baba was lying on the floor, not even moving.

"What happened to my Mother?" she said. "Is she sleeping on the floor? And why is her face covered up with her apron?"

"She's not asleep, Mom," I said. "She lay down and didn't move, so I covered up her face so we wouldn't have to look at her. I think she's dead."

"Dead? What do you mean dead?"

"Well, Baba yelled at me and I wished her dead," I blurted out, through tears welling in my eyes. Man, am I in trouble. Real trouble! "And, my wish came true."

"You can't wish someone dead, silly boy," Mom shook her

head, lifting the apron off her mother's head.

To which Baba yelled, "Fooled ya," and jumped to her feet.

Actually, she couldn't exactly jump to her feet. She rolled around on the floor and when she managed to balance on her hands and knees, she then hoisted herself up onto one foot and then the other, and then straight up. She was definitely not a spry chick.

I guess Baba was smarter than I gave her credit for. She just frowned, wrinkling her forehead and responded, "No way am I dying until it's my time, which should be when I'm around 100."

"But, Baba," I said, not feeling any better for making such a dumb and nasty wish. "I wished you dead. That's horrible. I'm really sorry."

"Don't worry, kid," she said, dismissing the whole thought. "Just to be even, sometimes I wish *you* would disappear. Forever. And yet, here you are – day in, day out – like a bad rash. And there is no vanishing cream in any cosmetic counter in all the department stores on earth that I could rub into your little bum – to make *my* wish come true – for you to disappear."

And then, in a sort of mocking way, she peered into my eyes and said with great vehemence, "I'll live long enough until I no longer can go to the bathroom by myself... and, *you*, heaven forbid, have to change *my* diaper."

To which I yelled out with just as much emphasis, "Yuk! Don't gross me out! I take it back, Baba. Please, let me take it all back. I want you to live forever!" I wanted to add, even if you're going to drive me crazy for the rest of my life!

But, for the time being, it seemed like all had been forgiven and I didn't want to start the process again by giving her an option of another nasty rebuttal.

Sometimes, Baba lived in a self-manufactured twilight zone.

She once told me that for two dollars, a palm reader in a tea shop on St. Catherine's Street, gazed into a crystal ball, and said that Baba – who was in her twenties at the time – would live to a ripe old age in her eighties. If she stopped smoking cigarettes and gave up drinking Sloe Gin Fizzes. Which was her favourite drink back in the '60s, when she lived and worked in Montreal.

I never saw her smoking cigarettes, so she must have given up the habit decades later. And now, instead of Sloe Gin Fizzes, she prefers red wine. And a generous nightly sip of sherry to clear away all the daily noise in her head generated by us brats, she'd say with a wink.

So, if the crystal ball reader was right, Baba should be around for more than twenty, maybe even thirty years. And she'd still be around to remind me to wash my hands!

Yikes!

THOU SHALT NOT TAKE GOD'S NAME IN VAIN

OMG: Oh my God – or is it Oh my gosh? Or golly? Or goody? So many variations in the dictionary or lexicon in the new-age of computer lingo.

The first time I said it, Baba let it pass. I'm on an iPOD game, and each time I zap my target in a quest of beating my opponent, I utter O! M! G! After several of these OMGs, Baba lit into me.

"Enough with the swearing about God. You should know better than to use God's name in vain."

Since I've never been to church or read the Bible, I didn't realize it was forbidden. After all, it was on the Internet. And everything on the Internet is true, isn't it? Surely the gurus who put out all that information validated accuracies before licensing the World Wide Web?

Baba says half of the stuff on the Internet is crap: her word, not mine.

"I know what I'm talking about," she said. "For years I keyed and verified customer sales information into a huge databank for that oil company I worked at."

According to Baba, the guys who created the Internet gave us a whole new world of information available to anyone, but not always accurate. Guys sat at their desks keying crap into computer programs – in the name of gathering informational data. Some never cross-checked with reference books for accuracies.

"All dictionaries, encyclopaedias and most reference books

are written by reliable writers, whose words are checked and rechecked by publishers to ensure that information was plausible and made sense."

"What does plausible mean?" My sister took her thumb out of her mouth long enough to ask, and then promptly returned it and continued sucking on it as she waited for Baba to explain.

"Plausible, little girl, is what I often don't think your brother is," she said with a smirk. "Especially, when he tells me he's sorry his foot slipped and he tripped you by mistake."

She continued, "If you're using religious terminologies in cussing, you should at least know where they came from. There's a movie I want you to watch," Baba said. "*The Ten Commandments* was an epic of huge proportion starring Charlton Heston, as Moses, who parted the Red Sea saving the good guys and drowning the bad guys – soldiers and their horses all drowned."

A few days later, Baba handed me a Bible. It was a small one in size, written specially for children. I'm going on ten, so I guess she still considers me a child.

For the next few weeks I read the Bible. I learned how the earth was created in six days and God rested on the seventh day.

Aha! Now I know why Baba refused to do any housework on Sundays – she also needed a well-deserved day of rest.

I read how the locusts destroyed the earth by eating up all the vegetation. How God raised his hand and cast fire and brimstone upon the people who did not obey him. And finally, there's proof that Baba was right – Delilah did cut off Samson's long locks and rendered him powerless. After he refused her advances – whatever that meant.

But, what was the purpose of turning what's-his-name's wife

into a pillar of salt – just because she looked back from whence she came? Really?

If God is all that loving and forgiving, why did He not let bygones be bygones and forgive her trespasses with a warning to never do what she was accused of doing. Anyway, in mythology it may be possible to turn a human into a pillar of salt, but in real life? I think not.

The story of Noah, however, was very confusing. What I don't get is how did the earth populate itself after the great flood when the Ark is saved from peril with all the animals and only Noah, his wife and two sons.

Now, I know enough about where babies came from to know you need a man's sperm and a woman's egg – and from that union, a woman carries a would-be baby in her stomach and nine months later – *voila!* another kid is wailing to become part of the universe. Just like my sister did when I was three.

So, as she was the only female on board, did Noah's wife give birth to children sired by her own sons? Would that not be a no-no? And, as she was the only female in the whole world she was the obvious one to carry on the population.

Maybe there was another Ark with another Noah and his wife – and two daughters. Now that would make sense to me. And this Ark met up with the real Noah and thus began the new world of Noahs and Noahs as the families mingled and begat a whole new world.

Maybe the guys who wrote the original Bible missed that opportunity to let readers know that not all are that gullible.

Maybe I should check on the Internet for an updated version of the Bible. Maybe these new writers would include the other Ark with two daughters, who married the original Noah's sons and they lived happily ever after with many children being bred to create a new world after forty days of flooding the earth, until both arks finally found dry land.

Some of the tales in the Bible I found almost as believable as the fairy tale movies produced by Walt Disney. Yet, events in the Bible were supposed to be as life actually happened, so not everyone had a happy ending.

When Athena was ten, Baba took her to see the new Noah epic with Russell Crowe. Apparently, this version was all about Noah and family felling trees and building an ark with long tree logs tied together to form a *huge* raft, with a roof. The Noahs hoped to board the ark and sail away before a swarm of alien-like non-humans got on board and killed them all – depriving the future world of human life.

Two by two, the animals, reptiles, birds, bugs and any and all forms of life were herded onto this raft with bales of hay and other eatables for the long voyage to seek dry land.

About a third into the movie, Baba and my sister walked out.

"It was not a movie I wanted to waste my Sunday afternoon on," Baba said.

"Yeah," said Athena, "I kept my hands to my ears to drown out the horrible noise."

"But the thing that really got to me was all the dirt!" said Baba. "Dirty clothes, filthy bodies with dirt all around. For forty days and forty nights they were at sea, with no land. So where did all that dirt come from? You'd think with all that rain flooding the world, there would be some water used to wash the dirt off their faces. Especially that filth from underneath their fingernails," Baba shuddered as if being grossed out.

I imagined Baba yelling at the screen, *Hey, Noah, wash your filthy hands! Again!*

"Make-up people probably spent more time putting dirt on their bodies than filming it," Baba said, shaking her head in disgust. "Anyway, it was a stupid movie, although it would have been interesting to be on the lot during the filming."

"Lessons learned, Baba," I said, recalling many times she reminded me of my wasted efforts with little result.

If truth be told, Baba said, not everything in the Bible should be taken as gospel. After all, the Bible was written by men who had nothing better to do with their leisure time than to drink mead, while making up parables and tales of what-ifs. Modern science has proven that many events depicted in the Bible defied logic and the probability of the world's creation according to the Bible is about a gazillion to none. Not logical. Never happened.

But, Baba says, we must have an open mind about things we cannot prove.

"You never know where you will end up after you die," she said. "So, it wouldn't hurt to somewhat believe in Heaven and Hell."

"So, Baba?" I asked her. "Are you going to Heaven or Hell when you die?"

"Makes no difference to me where I end up, kiddo." She shrugged her shoulders, scrunching up her face. "I'm lucky, I have friends in both places."

BABA'S TALE
– UKRAINE –
1944

RELIGIOUS BELIEFS

Sunday was our Sabbath and no one raised a tool, pitchfork or hoe or even a knife on Sunday.

On Saturday, Mama and my sisters cut up meat, potatoes and vegetables to cook in a huge pot for reheating on Sunday for our main meal after church.

A devout Christian family, we attended church services every Sunday in the Greek Orthodox Church in the nearby town of Komarivtsi. All through the Liturgy, which lasted at least two hours, we sang hymns, whispered prayers while kneeling on the hardwood floor, and crossed ourselves a lot. When we left the church, we felt confident that God forgave us whatever sins we may have committed during the previous week. And most of us felt we had a good chance of spending eternity in Heaven as the angels floated on puffy clouds, while strumming their harps. Eternal bliss for the duration of our alternate life in the hereafter. So the sermons promised us.

After church, back at home we enjoyed a hearty meal and a day of rest.

Each evening at bedtime, we knelt on our knees by our beds and said our prayers. Mostly we thanked God for our good life, our food and that we were still alive. Especially after the war broke out between

Adolf Hitler and Joseph Stalin – two horrible despots who wanted to rule the world.

Papa was very religious and crossed himself a lot.

If I had a choice, I would have given up religion altogether. All that kneeling and praying. And always asking God to forgive us our trespasses, whatever that meant. How many sinful acts can a little kid commit when half of the time I didn't know wrong from right. Religion. My God, who needed it?

Mama was just as religious, but instead of crossing herself as often as Papa did, she thumped her chest with a fist. With head slightly tilting up at the chin, she'd focus her eyes into the sky or ceiling depending on where she was, make a fist with her right hand and give her chest three thumps on the left side, just above her breast around the heart. Three thumps, not rapidly, just at an even tempo with a pause after each one. Thump... thump... thump.

Papa was a crosser and Mama was a thumper. Which was fine by me, except at times she took her beliefs too far and scared me with her stories of God's wrath and the horrible things that happen to people who did not pray to God each day and kept Sunday as a Sabbath.

One of those taboos involved working with machinery or equipment, like hammers, saws or nails. All were forbidden on Sunday. They were the tools and equipment that the sinners used to nail Jesus onto the cross, way back when. So each time you use a tool on Sunday, Mama said, we'd be nailing Jesus to the cross. Over and over again.

Another weird belief Mama threatened us with came about on a Sunday morning, as the family was preparing for church. Papa reminded Maria to run to the barn and secure the latch on the door. In her haste, Maria ripped the hem of her Sunday dress on a nail. She was about to thread a needle to mend the tear, when Mama lit into her.

*"Don't you dare put that thread through the hole in that needle!"
Mama yelled. "Do you know what curse God sends onto those who
don't worship him on Sundays?"*

*Curse? What curse? Why would God send a curse upon us for
using a thread and needle? Why is mending a rip a curse on Sunday?
Maria couldn't go to church in a torn dress. Would God send down
some of his angels to help with the mending? It would save her a lot of
work if He did. But He didn't. At least I never saw any angels threading
needles and mending rips and tears.*

*But, Mama knew best. Mama was an authority of how God and
his wonders worked. And sewing on Sunday was a blasphemous act.*

*The curse was that if you indulge in any form of sewing on Sunday,
when you die you must pass an obstacle course as a penance. If you
manage to squeeze your body through the eye of a needle, you will go to
heaven. If not, your soul will be damned to float aimlessly in purgatory
through eternity.*

*Can you imagine making yourself so thin that you would slide
through the eye of a needle?*

"You made that up, Mama."

*"Yes you did. Just to get away from work for at least one day a
week."*

"I'm not taking any chances," Petro said.

*"You don't need to worry. When was the last time you sewed any-
thing? You don't even know how to thread a needle."*

*"What if a button pops off when you are dressing for church on
Sunday morning? What do I do then?"*

"Then you wear something else," Mama said.

"What if nothing else is clean?"

"Then before you go to bed on Saturday, you make sure you have

another clean outfit."

"What if you forget? You're almost finished threading the needle and then you remember it's Sunday morning. What then?"

"Then you go to church and pray that God forgives you?"

The questions between my sisters and Mama went back and forth until they exhausted the theory of God's punishments.

But Mama had put the fear of God's wrath into me. Scared me off any idea of working on Sundays. Not that I ever had the urge to work. Any day, never mind just on a Sunday. But each time I had a vision of holding my breath to squeeze through the eye of a needle, a thin one for embroidering fine threads, I shuddered.

"But if God forgives me every time, I won't have to worry about not being skinny enough to fit through the needle when I die." Anna challenged Mama to the point of frustration.

"Yes, Anna," Mama said. "You won't ever have to worry about being skinny enough to wiggle through an eye of any size needle. As long as you don't sew on Sunday."

Poor Anna was petrified, being so overweight and all.

But she did not need to worry. For within a very short time, we'd all be thin enough to fit through the eye of a needle. Including Anna. And no way was it the result of sewing on Sundays. Starvation took care of that.

LOBSTER

Baba said only the rich people can afford to eat lobster.

"Years ago, lobster was used as a food for fish – ha, ha – and then it became a delicacy and the price rose and only those with higher incomes could afford it. Or, if it's a special occasion – like Birthday – then people splurged," she said.

"In mid-1960s, I was in a restaurant in Montreal. My three girlfriends and I ordered regular meals, but then I noticed a classy-looking lady dressed like only the rich did. In front of her was a platter with a huge red lobster and with great confidence, she dug the meat out of the shell with a special utensil, dipped it into melted butter and put it into her mouth. And then, the lady uttered this yum...yum...yum as she chewed. Not one drop of butter landed on her plastic bib with a picture of a lobster. She savoured it all.

"One day, I told myself I would be rich enough to look like that lady and eat lobster to my heart's content. "Then it happened," she said.

"You became rich!" I said.

"No! Not rich, but rich enough that I could afford lobster. Before I moved to B.C. from Ontario, I decided to drive out to Newfoundland. I sold most of my furniture and put a few things into a storage locker – to be shipped out when and where I decided to settle down again," Baba said.

"I packed my car with camera, laptop, maps, tape recorder and a trunk full of clothes and linens."

"You drove across Canada all by yourself?" I asked.

"I did."

"Weren't you afraid?"

"Sure, I was petrified. But your Uncle Dee encouraged me to go – said if I felt nervous on the highway, pull over, have a coffee, relax and then get back on the road and tell yourself 'I can do it.' Had I not gone, I'd have nothing to look back at. And no stories to tell you – ha, ha. I always wondered what it would have been like to drive across our country to see what's out there.

"So, I drove east to Montreal, then south to Vermont and New Hampshire. My first day in Maine I had lobster for dinner and lobster pancakes for breakfast the next morning. For two days, I ate lobster every meal. When I got on a ferry from Bar Harbour to Yarmouth my appetite for lobster was gone," she said, making a face as if she was full of food.

"I guess you can only eat so much lobster, eh?" I said.

"Yep, too much of anything – delicious as it may be – can be a turnoff," she said, nodding her head several times.

"But," she said with a grin, "this Christmas Eve we're having *surf 'n turf*. Your mom's Beef Wellington and dad is grilling lobster tails on the barbeque. Yummy."

YOU ARE ONE MIXED UP KID

"You don't need to waste money paying somebody else to tell you where you came from," Baba said when I asked her help to search out information for a family tree project I wanted to do to find out about my ancestors. Maybe I would finally validate all those stories about where Baba said she came from.

"But there's a program on the Internet and if we send them a hair or a spit on a tissue, they can tell us who were our great-greats going back to way before you can ever remember," I said.

"Listen, kid," Baba warned me. "You do not want some fly-by-night company knowing all about who you are and where you came from. No matter how reputable they say they are in keeping information about your private life safe.

"Anyway, to get accurate results, all members of your family have to submit their DNA. If one doesn't, the chain is broken and the results are skewed – and not complete. So, you're better off knowing what your relatives tell you what they remember."

"Okay," I said. "Can you at least tell me what you remember?"

"Sure, back in the 1960s, on your mother's side: Mary – your granddad's mother – had three children with her first husband, who died around – I think – age 30. Then she married John, a widower who also had three children. Their union together created seven sons and one daughter. So in total there were thirteen in that family. Three different marriages procreated fourteen siblings.

"Wow, that's a lot of kids," I said.

"French-Canadian families had many children – whether they wanted them or not," Baba said. "I married the eldest son from Mary and John's union. Your granddad Joe and I had two children: Uncle Dee and your mom."

"Over the next decade or so all the sons got married, had kids who also married when they grew up. As each generation aged, they married and created more children."

As a start, I would need to get in touch with, at least, 13 of my granddad's siblings – all living in various parts of *La Belle Province du Québec*. First I'd call or write asking questions like 'what was my cousin's name and when was s/he born?' And as they replied with names and dates of their children I would design a huge family tree.

When Baba started counting off the many, many number of second and third cousins that already exist just on my Mom's side, I realized it was way too big of a project to continue. Getting permission from everyone would probably take *way* more than two weeks. No way would I meet my project deadline and not be penalized for late submission.

"Or," Baba suggested an alternate route when it looked like I wasn't going to succeed, "I can give you all their names and based on their age now, we can do an approximate date of birth. Year anyway."

"What if some of the information is not very accurate," I asked. I didn't want my teacher to ask for proof of research.

"Tell her it's my fault," Baba said. "Anyway, even though the information should be accurate, for this project I would think steps of the process would be more important than the accuracy of date of birth of each person."

Turned out Baba was right. Since I only did my Mother's side, my family tree project only got me a B+.

"Excellent," Baba said. "And we did it the old-fashioned word-of-mouth way of research – without surfing the Net."

BABA'S TALE
– UKRAINE –
1944

PRELUDE TO WAR

It was early spring of 1944 and the last of the snow had melted. Alongside our house patches of green sprang up through the ground. In a day or two, the air would turn warm and with a strong sun, the bluebells would burst into bloom. The air smelled of fresh green grass and soon the fruit trees would bud, and give forth a sweet aroma of blossoms.

What started as a promise of another year that would yield us a plentiful crop was not meant to be.

For that year, no crops were harvested. No corn or wheat ground into flour at the mill.

When the fruit ripened on the branches, we would not be there to shake the trunk and gather ripe apples as they fell to the ground.

I had no idea what war meant. Not quite five, my only concern in life was watching Mama's pig as it lay in its pen and herding geese with a stick as they quacked through the cornfield.

The whispers among the grownups continued for months. I heard the word 'war' spoken many times. But when they noticed me hovering about, they stopped whispering.

"Papa, what is war?" I asked.

"Don't worry yourself about war, my dear Genia." Papa hugged me so tight that I thought he would break me in half.

"But why do you and the other grownups stop talking when they see me?"

"War is for grownups to think about. It has nothing to do with you children. You'd better get yourself off and see if those chickens laid any fresh eggs in the barn. My stomach is starting to growl from hunger."

Papa kissed the top of my head and patted me on my backside.

"Off you go now, shoo." He guided me towards the barn.

So off I went to collect eggs for our breakfast. Sure as daylight, the chickens always knew I was coming. As soon as I showed up, they danced around, squawking, wishing me a good day, so happy to see me.

"You silly goose, you," Anna said. "They're not happy to see you. They're trying to scare you off, telling you to get lost and stop stealing their eggs. They're protecting their young chicks."

"Yeah, every time you take an egg from a chicken, you are destroying a little chick that hasn't had a chance to hatch yet," said Maria.

"Then why do we take their eggs away from them, Papa?"

"Because we need to eat, my little one. We breed animals to survive."

"Yeah," Anna said, smacking her mouth with delight and rubbing her stomach. "Like fried bacon and delicious roasted veal."

But it would be many months, if not years, before Anna had a taste of fried bacon again.

MR. PETRENKO

Word travelled that Russian soldiers were going farm to farm and ordering landowners into trucks and transporting them to unknown places. No one knew where they were taken, as none came back to tell.

Papa said, "See child. This is what war is all about. It's about protecting what is yours. War is about greed and some will kill to take *what they want."*

Taking something that doesn't belong to you. I still didn't understand the reason for war.

Three days later, my question was answered.

It's the first few days of July 1944 and I got my first taste of war. In the early morning, an army truck screeched to a halt along the path of the Petrenko's farm. Two Soviet soldiers jumped out of the truck and headed towards the house.

"Open up! Open up!" They banged on the front door. Before Mrs. Saveta Petrenko had a chance to open it, the soldiers bolted inside. A few seconds later they dragged Saveta Petrenko and her two children outside.

Upon hearing the commotion, Mr. Petrenko came from the back of the house and faced the soldier.

"This is my land! You have no right to come on my property. No one can force me off my own land. You and your friends better leave now!" Mr. Petrenko yelled at the soldiers. In his hands he held a garden hoe. And as he ordered the soldiers to leave, Mr. Petrenko charged with the hoe, as if it were a sword as a brave Cossack would to defend himself. But Mr. Petrenko was no Cossack.

A slight man in his forties, he stood as tall as a cornfield and as thin as a rake.

No, Mr. Petrenko was no Cossack. Yet that morning he challenged the Soviet soldiers as if he were.

But he was no match for the Soviets who seized farms and ordered the peasants onto trucks.

"Please Ivan," his wife tugged at his sleeve, begging him not to defy the soldiers. "Please Ivan, just do what they say."

But proud Mr. Petrenko stood his ground.

"Quiet woman, let me deal with this. You go back in the house and take the children with you."

As Saveta Petrenko turned towards the house, a shot rang out. At the sound of the crack of a pistol, she spun around.

Mr. Petrenko clutched his chest and stumbled forward, towards his assailant. Without moving a single step, the soldier took another aim and fired another shot. Mr. Petrenko's knees buckled under, and as his body dropped to the ground, another bullet pierced his body. Blood oozed out of Mr. Petrenko's chest and the ground around him was bright red. The second soldier aimed his pistol and fired once. For assurance. In case the body on the ground would somehow come to life. Maybe even threaten him. Four bullets in total were fired. Poor Mr. Petrenko didn't stand a chance of surviving.

The Russian soldiers lifted Mr. Petrenko's dead body off the ground and pitched it into the back of the army truck. And they ordered Saveta Petrenko and her two children to climb in with the dead body of her husband. Saveta Petrenko wailed in despair. But the plea for mercy out of her throat was cut in mid-scream as the soldier slammed a rifle butt to her head.

Mama gasped in horror and stuffed the corner of her apron into her mouth to stifle a scream. Her body started to vibrate and she wept, ever so silently. With one hand she held the apron. And the other hand clutched me tightly against the back of her legs, wrapping me in the folds of her peasant skirt for protection.

But I couldn't take my eyes off what was happening. In just a few seconds, the Russian Communists killed our neighbour and dragged the rest of his family away.

"You!" yelled the soldier pointing a pistol at my father.

At the sound of the soldier's voice, Papa jammed a pitchfork into the ground and leaned on it.

"You are next on our list for evacuation. We'll be back for you and your family!"

"But we are not ready to leave," Papa boldly announced. He looked *straight into the soldier's eyes.*

It was the same soldier who just a few minutes earlier shot and killed Mr. Petrenko, Papa's neighbour and his friend of so many years. And now he was no more. Just a crumpled up dead body.

Gone are the relaxing evenings when Papa and Mr. Petrenko sat together in the cool shade of an oak tree as they often did, after a hard day's work in the fields.

Now, Papa was defying the soldiers who had killed his best friend and taken Saveta Petrenko and their children away in a truck to only God knew where. Perhaps to toil on collective farms, or a slave camp in Siberia. Or be shot and thrown into a pit filled with other dead bodies and be sprayed with acid to burn and dissolve the rotting flesh.

"Nobody asked you if you are ready," yelled the soldier. "It's fortunate for you that the truck is full. We have orders to gather all able bodies for a work detail. In a few days, we will be back for you and your family. Ready or not, you are next on our list."

The choices were not theirs to make. The soldiers had their orders and if they didn't carry them out, they too would be shot. Or sent off to prison.

The truck carrying the Petrenkos raced down the road in a cloud of dust.

"We will never see them again," Papa said to Mama.

"What are we to do?"

"We must leave."

"Leave? Leave our home? Where would we go?"

"We cannot let this happen to us. They will not take us alive. For we must survive their terror."

Papa was strong in his belief, but only time would tell if we'd live to talk about it.

COSSACKS

"What about the Cossacks, Papa! Let's wait for the Cossacks. They will come and rescue us," I said. "Won't they, Papa?"

The Cossacks were my heroes. Papa entertained us with many stories about the good they had done for the people of Ukraine. An army of skilled swordsmen, the Cossacks rode strong and fast horses. When the sound of hoofs clippity-clopped over cobble-stoned roads, the Cossacks were on a mission of good deeds. And anyone who threatened the security of peasant farms or city dwellers met their fate at the tip of the Cossack sword.

For centuries the "good" Cossacks fought the "bad" ones to protect Ukraine and its people and land. So, I was sure that any time soon a band of "good" Cossacks would come to our rescue. They would ride their horses at top speed and with their swords held high, cut the "bad" Russian soldiers in half.

"Not this time, my child," Papa said, wiping tears from his face. "This time even the Cossacks can't save us. Not from Stalin. That monster who orders soldiers to torch homes and shoot anyone who got in their way."

I had never before seen such a sad look of despair on Papa's face.

Papa was right. The Cossacks never came. No one came to save us.

"My God, my God," said Papa, blessing himself. "Those Bolsheviks torched our church in town. They will stop at nothing and destroy everything."

"Dyonisis," said Mama. "We cannot stay here. It is no longer safe. I am afraid for our lives. Please Dyonisis, we must leave to save ourselves. Think of our children."

"But where will we go, Olena? There is no haven safe from the clutches of those Bolsheviks."

"What will happen to us if we stay?"

"They will come tomorrow morning and get us. Like they said they would. Load us into the truck and take us away to only heaven knows where."

THE NIGHT BEFORE

That evening after supper, we gathered in the kitchen for a family meeting.

When you're the youngest in a family of eight, quite often grownups don't waste much time explaining things. So I really didn't know what was happening. But from the way they all talked, I knew we were in deep trouble.

"We have one day to decide what we must do," Papa said. His voice trembled as he stared out the window. He pretended to be in control and spoke with authority. Yet, he himself had no way of knowing our destiny. Or, if what he ordered us to do was for our best.

"We can no longer stay. The soldiers will be back. They will take us away, whether we are ready or not. We have no choice but to gather our belongings and head for the hills."

"The hills?" Mama said. "What hills are you talking about?"

"The mountains. We must escape through the Carpathians and pray to God that we get to the Romanian border before those Russians realize we are missing."

"We are escaping to Romania? It will take days – if not weeks – for us to cross the mountains."

"No, Papa." Petro stood tall, flexing his muscles. "We can't leave our home. We'll stay and fight."

"Are you crazy?" Papa said, and smacked his forehead with the palm of his hand. "You think you have the strength to fight machine guns and tanks?"

"We must try, Papa. They can't drive us out of our home. We'll gather all the men off the farms and fight those Bolsheviks."

"If they catch us, Petro, you just may get your chance to fight. How would you like to join the Russian Army, eh? They will give you a rifle and order you to shoot any Christian that got in your way. And if you don't, off they haul you to Siberia. Or, shoot you themselves."

"Oh, my God. What if they force you to shoot us?" said Maria.

"There is no other way, we must save our lives. Tomorrow at dusk, we leave and make our way towards the mountains overnight."

"And if we make it safely to Romania?" Mama pleaded with Papa. "What then? Where will we go?"

"I don't know what we'll do then, Olena. We'll put our destiny into God's hands."

"What's the worst that can happen to us if we stay, Papa?" said Elizabeth.

"The worst? Well, if I had my choice between concentration camp and death, I'd take death. Being shot would be a blessing. All of us thrown into pits to join all the other dead Ukrainians. Like they killed Ivan Petrenko. Right in front of his wife and children. Murderers!"

"My dear husband, please don't talk like that. You're scaring the young ones."

"As much as I want to I can't stop what's happening. The whole world is at war. No one is safe anymore."

"But if we stay, maybe the Russians will let us work our farm. I heard that some of the farmers are willing to stay and work the land. Even the Russians need wheat and corn and cattle to feed their armies."

"That may well be true, but we will lose our freedom. Our farm will become Communist property and all crops would go to them. They will eat our bread and meat. And we would starve."

"Why don't we vote, Papa? If we all want to remain here, then we

should," Anastazia suggested.

"You want to vote?" Papa said. "We'll vote? Yes to stay. No to go."

And the votes began. Raise your right hand for yes, your left hand for no.

No, no, yes, no, no, yes, no, yes.

Anastazia voted to stay on the farm with her baby, and wait for her husband to return from the war front.

Petro claimed he could whip any Russian and wanted the chance to prove his manhood.

I voted yes, even though I had no idea what I was saying yes to. Papa said if there is a tie, we'd vote again. We would have kept on voting over and over until there were enough no votes. Papa had no intention of staying behind. So his democracy ruled in our household.

In a day or two, the Communist soldiers would be knocking down our door. If we hurried, we might get out before they showed up.

And so we prepared to evacuate.

We packed bread, chunks of salted and smoked meats, fruit and vegetables into sacks and pillowcases. We dressed ourselves in layers of clothing and took with us whatever we could carry. At the crack of dawn, Papa closed the door to our straw-thatched home for the last time.

We left fields full of corn, rye and wheat stalks protruding through the soil but we would not reap the harvest that year. Nor the next year. Never again to stand atop a hill and inhale the sweet smell of clover as fields brought forth their buds.

Little baby apples and plums were just beginning in the summer sun. Never again would we bite into a ripe, succulent plum or pear plucked right off the tree in our orchard.

"Did we leave anyone behind?" Papa asked, as we walked along a

path away from our home.

"One, two..." Mama started counting and when she got past eight she said, "Nine. No, no one left behind. We are all here."

As we snuck away through the fields and headed towards the forest in the Carpathian Mountains, we prayed that the Russian Communists would not catch up to us.

But, they did.

HAIR CUTS

"Who cut your hair?" Mom asked when Baba showed up with new streaks and a little lopsided haircut.

"I woke up this morning with one hair too long, took scissors and before I knew it – snip here snip there and voila, I'm my own barber."

"Sure looks like it," I heard Mom mumble to herself as she shook her head.

"Oh, yeah?" Baba said. "Well, the last time I had a professional style my hair I had to trim around my ears because she thought I would look better with sideburns. Well, I don't! Sideburns are for men, not women. Anyway if it doesn't stay put against my face, it flies every which way. As long as I can face myself in the mirror..."

Baba was all dressed up in a red and black jacket and black slacks, with matching black velvet knee-high boots.

"Where are you off to?" Mom said.

"The Art Gallery," Baba said. "Going to see if my two pairs of leisure socks got a bid."

The Public Art Gallery was having a fundraiser to help build homes for the less fortunate.

Habitat for Humanity is an organization started years ago by Linda and Millard Fuller, and supported by Jimmy Carter, former president of United States of America. Their idea of communities contributing towards helping those in need of a home to live was huge, with many countries around the world taking part.

Donations of art works of any form were displayed in the Gallery for a silent auction. It was a social event with many artists offering a piece of their work to be auctioned off.

"Come with me?" Baba said to Mom. "It'll be like a mother and daughter evening out and maybe later we can go out for a drink."

"Sorry, Mom. Alex and I have soccer tonight."

"You spend way too much time with your brats," Baba said and winked at me.

I played soccer for the local team and Mom was one of our coaches.

So off Baba went to her event and a few days later she showed up with a photo of her leisure socks hanging by strings on display at the Art Gallery.

"There was a bidding war for my contribution to the silent auction," Baba boasted. "Well, actually, there were just two bids. In the end, someone paid $75 for two pairs of my leisure socks."

"Told you your socks were great," Mom said. Baba always needed confirmation that her knits were well made and good for the public to buy.

"If only my hair was that great, eh?" Baba said, reminding Mom what she said about her hair the last time she was here.

"Actually, your hair doesn't look half bad." Mom said. "Now that it's grown out a bit and with the blond streaks, it looks fine."

"Thanks, kid," Baba said and with a grin she added, "Maybe now as a blonde, I'll have more fun, eh?"

DEBATES

"If you really must question every order I give you," Baba said, "make yourself useful and join the Debating Club at school."

"Really? What would I debate about?"

"Anything and everything that you may not agree with, have a question about or even want to stir the you-know-what in another person," she said. "Your options of a subject to debate are limitless."

"Like what?" I asked. "Give me an example."

"Like…" she started to say and then did that thing where she rolls her eyes and looks up to see if maybe someone had written the answer up there on the ceiling.

"Doesn't a debate have to be about something really serious, like war or hunger or more timely like global warming?"

"Grass. That's it, kid," she said with a big smile. "There's your answer."

"Grass?"

"Yep, you should have a debate about a blade of grass," she said, nodding her head, satisfied that at least her idea was somewhat sound.

A debate about a single blade of grass? Really?

Actually, when I gave it some serious thought over the next few days, a debate about a blade of grass could bring up a whole list of issues.

Reasons for growing blades of grass – food for cows, who provide beef and milk and hide for leather. Without a single blade of grass – we might just starve. Very interesting. Maybe the old Baba's brain is not yet out of whack as I often thought it was.

Grass keeps the dirt from flying all over the atmosphere, etc. Without grass, we'd be walking barefoot on lawns made up of – ouch – ouch – ouch – dirt and gravel. And most important for us kids, no rolling down hills covered by gazillions of soft luscious blades of green grass.

Unfortunately, my school did not have a debating club. After speaking with a couple of my teachers, they recommended if I wanted to start one I should make a presentation on how to create a debate club to the School Board. Turned out by the time it took me to come up with a half-decent plan, it was June and school was out.

Maybe when I get to University I just might put Baba's test of why I should debate a single blade of grass.

HIGH SCHOOL

Fast forward to the present. At twelve, I passed the babysitting course and my dumb sister – who spent most of her growing years sucking her thumb – turned out to be not so dumb after all with a B+ and all others As, in her first year of High School – no longer needed her Baba.

For several years, I had been in charge of my sister when our parents went out. Athena and I have finally grown up – sort of. On the verge of growing up. But we definitely enjoyed being independent and not have Baba ordering us around on what to do and where not to go.

Yet, I know there have been many times when Athena wished for me to disappear. And her Baba to show up at our front door, announcing herself with that so-familiar, "Hello, kiddies. It's me. I'm heeere."

And Mom was right. Sort of. Looking back, life did fly by, before I knew it.

Now more than a decade later, my last year in High School I have first-day jitters – like I've always had when September rolled around and another school year began.

As I entered my designated homeroom, I sat down at an empty desk.

Standing in front of a huge chalkboard stood a gorgeous girl. Or lady, or whatever the legal term of the opposite of my gender are called nowadays. She stood tall, her long blond hair rolled up into a bun that perched on top of her head, like my kid sister often did when she danced ballet at recitals.

I thought this beauty was a classmate, buttering up the teacher on the first day by cleaning the chalkboard. But, it turned out she was the educator whose job was to lead me on my road to adulthood success.

"I am your home teacher for this year," said Teach. "You will address me as Ms. Fuller or Ma'am. You will never call me anything other."

"Especially not call you a girl – lady – woman – female?" My mouth opened and the words flew out. And in that split second, I heard Baba's nagging voice, "Should have let those words filter through the brain's censor board before they came out of your mouth, young man!"

Ms. Fuller peered at me through reading glasses perched on her nose and before she could chastise me, I said, "I apologize. I'm sorry. Must be first day jitters. You know. Like. Sorry. Really sorry."

"And you are?" she said and with a somewhat accusatory look she peered at me.

"Alexandre Sasha Davidson, Ma'am."

"So, Mr. Davidson. Are you auditioning for the role of the class clown?"

"No... not really. Unless you want me to be?" I said.

A couple of kids started to snicker and at the sound of chuckles, a tiny humph escaped Ms. Fuller as she turned towards the chalkboard. And at the very top, right-hand side, she wrote my name.

"Excuse me, Ms. Fuller," I interrupted. "Alexandre is spelled with an re not er. To reflect my French heritage."

"And I suppose Sasha is to reflect your Russian heritage?" she asked.

"Russian? Oh, my God, no! Heaven forbid – not Russian," I said, and rapidly my hand flew up, tap... tap... tap... tap... First my forehead, then chest, then right shoulder and, with a sign of relief, the left shoulder. Just like I watched Baba do every time she felt the need to ask God to shoo away the demons.

"Did you just cross yourself?" Ms. Fuller removed her reading glasses off her nose, and let them hang down on what looked like pink twisted knitting yarn that formed a chain wrapped around her neck.

"Ukrainian," I blurted out, hoping she would not focus on the one form of religion I happened to copy and from time to time used to emulate Baba. Just to make sure I ward off the devils that might be lurking around me.

"My middle name is Sasha. Although linguistically, it could be used in either language. Actually, nowadays many ethnic groups name their kids Sasha. In fact, our French-Canadian Prime Minister had a brother called Sasha. Sadly, he died in a skiing accident years ago. At least, that's what my Baba told me."

While I'm talking Ms. Fuller frowned, heaved a loud sign and looking up into the ceiling, she waited for me to finish my yada... yada... yada...

"No," I finally said. "It's definitely not Russian. It's Ukrainian – after my Mom's side."

"Detention, Mr. Davidson." Ms. Fuller corrected the spelling of my name on the chalkboard. "At 3 o'clock, sharp."

Really? Not even the sound of the end of the first period bell and already I'm in trouble? Is Teach going to be as harsh as Baba? Reincarnate of the Old Lady? Geeezzz!

"What if I have to pick up my kid sister from school," I asked, hoping she'd take back the detention, even though I was not in charge of my sister.

"Then you should have thought of your responsibilities before you opened your mouth."

You got me there, Teach.

"Now," Ms. Fuller walked to the left side of the chalkboard, "welcome to Grade 12 – your last year of coddling by your parents and the education system."

As she talked, she turned towards the chalkboard and continued writing.

"At the end of this school year, all of you will be considered adults. Almost. Some of you may have grown up into adulthood during the last four years and some of you may not," she said.

"Whatever you choose to do from now on, you alone will be responsible for your actions – good or bad. Some of you will go right into the work force and others on to university or trade school."

Then looking straight at me as if I were the only one in the classroom, she said with a chuckle, "It's even possible that one of you might join the improv circuit to become a comedian."

Chuckle... chuckle... snicker... snicker... Several students muttered and then all was quiet again.

"I need to know what makes you young people tick," she said. "Your first written assignment is about the one person who influenced you most during your life so far," she said. "Think back to the day you were born – if you can remember that far back. If you can't, ask your parents. Who was there for you while you were growing up? A sports coach, your best friend or a relative.

It really doesn't matter who you write about, but what and how you write it, is."

She then read out loud what she had written on the chalk-board – just to make sure that we understood what she expected of us.

Subject: a memorable person who had an influence on your life

2,000 words – use word count

Full name: printed right-hand corner

Format: proper printing or typed – one inch margins all around

Due date: one week from today – NO EXCUSES

"After that date," she said, shaking her head, "I will not read it, so don't even bother handing it in. And your mark is an F."

"What if my Grandmother dies and I have to go to her funeral?" I ask, hoping to buy some time – just in case I need it.

"Is your grandmother ill, Mr. Davidson?"

"No, not yet." I know I'm pushing it, but I already have a de-tention, so I have nothing to lose.

"People die everyday. Would your grandmother want you to fail? Take three days to mourn and four days left to write your assignment. Life goes on, Mr. Davidson."

At her logic, I had no further rebuttal.

"This is our first of many writing assignments," Ms. Fuller con-tinued. "You may notice I did not say your assignment – because it's ours. You write, I read and mark it. And if I don't think your words are worthy of a good mark... well, it's all up to you. You get what you earn. At least, what I think you deserve."

Really? One week to write 2,000 words. That's like at least 10 pages of a *Dork* book.

Who has influenced me the most so far? Hmmm. My track coach in grade school? My music teacher? Definitely my music teacher. Mom? Dad? My best friend... so far?

At the sound of dismissal bell for the first period, all students rush out of the classroom.

"Mr. Davidson," Ms. Fuller called out, "see you back here at 2:50."

"Yes, Ma'am," I managed and walked out to meet my best friend waiting for me in the hallway.

The rest of the first day was uneventful. At 2:50 I returned to my homeroom.

"So," Ms. Fuller looked up, sitting at her desk. "What should we do for our first detention, Mr. Davidson?"

"Er, actually, it's my detention. Not yours."

"True, but I must remain in class for the duration. Or at least for the next fifteen minutes until your punishment is over."

"Well, I could watch the clock."

"Watch the clock?" she said with a frown. "What purpose would that serve?"

I opened my mouth to tell Ms. Fuller about all the stories Baba told me how many times she was sent to the school principal's office or sat at her desk after class ended. As the minute hand ticked along round and around, she waited impatiently until her fifteen minutes was up and she was allowed to leave and go home.

Sometimes, Baba said, when she questioned the teacher to give her a good reason why she was given a detention, her penance became duplicates of fifteen minutes, spent sitting at her desk, after school, watching the clock – tick... tock... tick... tock.

On second thought, I picked up a pencil and started to write in my notebook.

"Time," Ms. Fuller finally announced. "You may leave, Mr. Davidson."

"See your tomorrow, Ms. Fuller." I forced a grin and walked out of the classroom.

As I strolled along the corridor, past lockers that would hold our books and who knows what else for my last year, I made a mental note to hold back my tongue. Speak when spoken to. And, as Baba often said, "It's better to keep your mouth shut and let them think you're stupid, than to open it and prove it."

Although, judging by her non-stop tales of her past, I'm sure Baba's been wrong many times.

And yet, I wonder if I should keep my detention – especially on the first day – to myself. And not divulge my penance of watching the clock, so she'd have nothing on me. Like she did all those times when I misbehaved and yelled at her to get out of our house! Even though my parents insisted that she was needed to look after my baby sister and me for way too many years. In my opinion.

And here I am, no longer needing Baba to take me to school. Or make me grilled cheese sandwiches while a friend visits for a play day. Nor to remind me to wash my hands as soon as I walk into the house. Actually, she drummed it into my brain so often that I automatically go to the sink when I come home.

Outside the school, I turn my phone on, and as if reading my mind, there's a text from you-know-who.

"How was school?"

Is she kidding? Will she ever leave me alone? I was about to text back, then realized I'd have to mention my detention, and then listen to her rant.

Did I not teach you anything? Speak when you're spoken to. You'll never get a scholarship to McGill or McMaster, young man! Forget MIT or Harvard.

I could hear that voice going on and on, rhyming off names of all the prestigious universities of the world. The ones she never qualified for with barely passing high school marks and reminded me so many times that I had the smarts to achieve anything I wanted if I put my mind to what really matters in life.

Instead, I send her a short text message of *great, but scary*.

To which she replied with a heart-shaped emoji: *well, if you need me – u know where I live. luv ya, Baba.*

BABA'S TALE
– UKRAINE –
1944

THE CARPATHIAN MOUNTAINS

The Carpathians are a mountain range in Central Europe extending from north Czechoslovakia to central Romania. About 900 miles in length, their highest peak is 8,737 feet.

Papa said our only salvation was through the Carpathian Mountains into Romania and then on to West Germany. As war refugees, we'd have protection from Stalin and his armies.

"We must at least try to escape," Papa said. "We will not become slaves to those monsters! We will not assimilate with their way of communist life."

"But what if we get caught?"

"Then heaven help us," Papa said, looking way up into the heavens and crossing himself. As always, three times.

When Papa and Mama took us through the mountains, I thought we were going on a camping trip. And after a few days in the woods, we'd return to the comfort of our home.

"Don't talk, don't even whisper. For even the trees have ears and they are not so friendly."

"Papa, why are we crouching so close to the ground? Why can't we romp through the woods? Let's build a bonfire and roast some potatoes like we do at home? Come on, Petro, play your balalaika. Let's dance,

Papa." I never got answers to all my questions.

"Shhh," Papa said. "Don't talk, child. Save your strength, for you'll need it later."

"Mama, why are we hiding? Why are you covering me up with bushes?" Mama gently covered my mouth with her hand and whispered into my ear. Slowly she settled into a grove of bushes, cradling me in her arms so close that I thought she might choke me. But I knew that she was trying to protect me from some kind of harm, so I settled into the warmth of her bosom and closed my eyes.

Papa had the wisdom to bring along a hatchet for chopping long branches to hide under while we slept in the cool evenings.

Lucky there were numerous lakes and ponds, so we were able to draw water to drink.

After a while, sleeping in the woods under brush was no longer a game.

For days, Mama had carefully doled out chunks of dry meats or smoked fat and bread. But soon we were down to just crumbs of stale bread and resorted to hunting the woods for edible greens. And in another day, there wouldn't even be any crumbs left to share between the eight of us. We ached for the comforts of our home and the plentiful life we once enjoyed.

"What I wouldn't do for a slice of soft fresh bread right out of our oven."

"Yeah, oozing with melted butter and sweetened by thick home-made plum jam."

"Don't even think about it."

"Papa, I'm hungry," I begged. "Why can't I have a slice of bread? Please, Papa, let's go back home. There must be eggs piled up high in the chicken coop. The chickens must be wondering why I'm not there to

pluck the eggs away, to make room for them to lay more."

"Hush child," Papa whispered as he hugged me close to himself to muffle the sound of my voice.

It would be weeks, months, before I ever tasted an egg again.

MARIA'S DREAM OF OUR CAPTURE

During our quest for freedom, Ukrainian partisans aided families who left their homes, seeking a new life. In another country? Albeit a foreign one. Or, wherever? Only God knew our destiny.

After a week of trekking through the mountains, one morning Maria woke up with startling news.

"I had a dream, Papa," she said. "A dream of our lives being in grave danger."

"Oy, Maria," Papa said. "Of course we are in grave danger. How much worse do you think it can be?"

Papa often dismissed Maria's wild and ominous visions as just another one of her need for seeking attention. He was sceptical to heed her advice, even though her prediction of leaving our home had come to pass.

But we had no farm to gather wheat from or milk a cow or hoe a garden patch. Our lives were reduced to an idle life – if one could have said human survival during a world war was an idle life.

"So, tell us about your wild visions, Maria." Papa said and gave his time to listen to her dream – perhaps her prophesy of our fate.

Just when we thought we crossed over the Romanian border into Austria and reached safety, we heard a loud HALT!
Blocking the pass were two army trucks. We had walked

right into a trap, set by Soviet soldiers. There was no need for them to trek the mountains to capture us. All they had to do was wait until we came out of the woods into the clearing. If we ran, we would surely all be shot. There was nowhere for us to go.

Upon orders, we climbed into the trucks. Papa herded us so that we at least stayed together. As the driver turned the truck heading east, back towards Ukraine, we huddled in the back. We were doomed. Our efforts were in vain.

But Maria was not about to give in without a fight.

"No! No! No!" she screamed as loud as she could and banged on the back of the driver's seat.

"Shut her up!" yelled the Soviet driver to the soldier sitting in the front passenger seat. Obeying the driver's command, he turned towards the back of the truck and lifted the flap that separated them. He was about to order the young girl to stop screaming, when he recognized her face and abruptly turned back towards the road.

"Oh my God, Mama, that's Yuri!" Maria said. "He's sitting up front next to the driver of the truck."

Yuri was the youngest son of George and Evhenia Shemchenko. Theirs was the farm that Soviet soldiers had occupied a few days earlier. Yuri had been forced into the Russian Army. The farmer's young son that Maria swore she'd never go out with was now taking us back to our farm. To work for the Communists or perish in a labour camp.

But Maria had no intentions of going back. "Yuri, please," she banged with her hands on the partition. "Please save us. Don't let them take us back."

"If you don't shut her up, I will!" The Soviet driver

again ordered Yuri to stop Maria but she continued plead-
ing with Yuri. Her screams became deafening.

"If you want her dead, you do it yourself!" Yuri yelled
back at the driver.

In anger, the driver screeched the truck to a halt,
opened the door and as he stepped down to the ground,
he pulled out his revolver. In a split second, a shot rang out
and the Soviet soldier lay dead on the ground.

"God, forgive me," Yuri said, as he dropped his
smoking revolver to the floor of the truck.

Fortunately, the other truck was ahead of them and no
one saw what had happened.

Swiftly, Yuri alit from the cabin and ran around to the
back of the truck.

"Hurry!" he said to Maria, and extended his hand.
"Come with me."

Maria hesitated, but when she realized that Yuri was
alive and the pistol shot was not meant for him, she said in
shock, "Did you kill the German driver?"

"There is no time to waste," Yuri said. "You must trust
me. Hurry before they miss the truck!"

Without thinking further, Maria jumped out of the
truck into Yuri's extended arms. With speed he hoisted
her into the passenger seat and ran around to the driver's
side. He put the truck in gear and instead of continuing
on the same route back to Ukraine, he turned the wheel to
the right and headed west towards Hungary, Austria and
Germany.

And as far away from Stalin as half a tank of petrol
would get him.

Ahead of us lay a long journey. But we were prepared to continue fighting Stalin and his soldiers. We had no other choice.

"Freedom," Papa said, "is life. Without freedom, there is no reason to live."

"Amen," said Mama. And with tears in her eyes, she looked up into the heavens and thumped her chest with her fist. Three times, as always. Thump... thump... thump...

Then Papa fell to his knees and crossed himself. Once... twice... thrice.

"That dream, Papa," Maria pleaded, "it told me what may happen to us. If it is our destiny, we must be very careful where we go next."

"Such a wild dream, Maria," Papa said and gave her a loving embrace. "But, God willing, if you are right, we may all survive. And you might live long enough to tell your grandchildren all about it."

The Tschoban Family - July 1945
At the end of World War II in Munster, Germany

Back row (from left): Cousin, Elizabeth, John (Immigration Guide),
Dyonisis, Olena, Anastazia, Albin (baby), Dmytro.

Front row (from left): Anna, Ewheniya - Jennie, Cousin, Cousin, Maria.

ACKNOWLEDGEMENTS

Thank you...

To my writing group of Martha, Ross, Nora, Mira and Natania; to all the people who attended Open Mics at the Gibsons Public Library and Art Gallery; to Sheila Cameron, Sharon Danroth and Weegee Sachtjen.

To Jan DeGrass, critic and editor – who offered valuable suggestions and edited my manuscript.

To my son Darrin, Kindrey and Lauren – where I earned my Nanny certificate while living with them for a year in Ontario.

To Russ, my son-in-law and April-Ria, my daughter. For more than ten years they trusted me with their most precious possessions – their son and daughter. The subjects of my memoir. Without them, I'd have nothing to write about.

Finally, to all my Ukrainian family and especially to Anna and Anastazia who often fought with each other – during my interviews – as they recalled the events of life in Ukraine during World War II – *Nazdorovlia...*

ABOUT THE AUTHOR

Jennie Choban – aka Ewheniya Tschoban – the youngest of six children, was born in Ukraine at the start of World War II.

In 1944, her family fled their home while Stalin's communist army fought for world control.

After spending five years in a Displaced Persons Refugee Camp in Germany, her family immigrated to Canada.

Jennie was schooled in Quebec, married and raised her children in Ontario and retired to the Sunshine Coast of British Columbia.

Jennie loves to travel and drove solo across Canada dipping her feet into the Atlantic and Pacific Oceans. And, she has photos to prove it.

Now that her grandkids are too old for her to baby sit, Jennie reads and knits socks and slippers for those who don't even want any.

Jennie's next project is to complete writing her novel.

Made in the USA
Monee, IL
28 November 2020